DOSTOIEVSKY: AN INTERPRETATION

NICOLAS BERDYAEV

Dostoievsky
An Interpretation

⊕

New Foreword *Boris Jakim*
Translator *Donald Attwater*

SEMANTRON PRESS

San Rafael CA

First Edition, Sheed & Ward, New York, 1934
Second, enlarged edition, Semantron Press 2009
Semantron is an imprint of Sophia Perennis LLC
New Foreword and Biography © Boris Jakim 2009

For information, address:
Semantron Press, P.O. Box 151011
San Rafael, CA 94915
semantronpress.com

Library of Congress Cataloging-in-Publication Data

Berdiaev, Nikolai, 1874–1948.
[Mirosozertsanie Dostoevskago. English]
Dostoievsky: an interpretation / by Nicolas Berdyaev;
[translated by Donald Attwater];
with a new foreword by Boris Jakim.

p. cm.
ISBN 978 1 59731 261 5 (pbk: alk. paper)
1. Dostoyevsky, Fyodor, 1821–1881—Criticism and interpretation.
2. Dostoyevsky, Fyodor, 1821–1881—Philosophy.
I. Attwater, Donald, 1892–1977. II. Title.
PG3328.B42 2009
891.73'3—dc22   2009022489

Cover photograph by Dorlys Paris

CONTENTS

NEW FOREWORD i

TRANSLATOR'S NOTE 5

FOREWORD 7

CHAPTER I. Spirit 11

CHAPTER II. Man 39

CHAPTER III. Freedom 67

CHAPTER IV. Evil 89

CHAPTER V. Love 111

CHAPTER VI. Revolution. Socialism 133

CHAPTER VII. Russia 160

CHAPTER VIII. The Grand Inquisitor. Christ and
   Antichrist 188

CHAPTER IX. Dostoievsky and Us 213

A BRIEF OVERVIEW of Nikolai Berdyaev's Life & Works 228

BIBLIOGRAPHY of Nikolai Berdyaev's Books in English 235

FOREWORD TO NEW EDITION

"So great is the worth of Dostoevsky that to have produced him is by itself sufficient justification for the existence of the Russian people in the world" (p. 227, present volume). This is Nikolai[1] Berdyaev's assessment of Fyodor Dostoevsky (1821–1881), the great Russian novelist, religious thinker, and prophet. Berdyaev states at the beginning that his task in *Dostoevsky: An Interpretation* is not to tackle his subject from a psychological angle. Rather, his aim is to examine Dostoevsky's spiritual side, to explore in all its depth the way in which Dostoevsky perceived the universe and to reconstruct out of these elements his entire world-view. Dostoevsky was not a psychologist, as many readers think, but a "pneumatologist," a symbolistic metaphysician. He was a "mystical-realist." (pp. 26–27, present volume).

Dostoevsky shows us new worlds, worlds in motion, by which alone human destinies can be made intelligible; and these worlds and these destinies can only be grasped by a spiritual analysis.[2] Essential to Dostoevsky's vision of the world is the role ideas play in human life: "For Dostoevsky, ideas are fiery billows, never frozen categories; they are bound up with the destiny of man, of the world, of God himself. They determine these destinies" (p. 12, present volume). Ideas are so paramount in Dostoevsky that there is in his works very little

---

1. "Nikolai" is the more correct form of Berdyaev's first name. The original translations of Berdyaev's works into English used "Nicolas"; in order to avoid confusion this spelling is retained on the cover and title page.

2. First published in 1923, this book was written in Moscow at the height of revolutionary fighting, when gunfire was rattling in the streets outside the window of Berdyaev's study, thus allowing him to experience first-hand the struggles of freedom and the creation of new worlds, forming human destinies. For Berdyaev too, the important thing was the spiritual side of the events.

i

recreation of the exterior world. His novels are not, properly speaking, novels at all. "They are parts of a tragedy, the inner tragedy of human destiny, the unique human spirit revealing itself in its various aspects and at different stages of its journey" (p. 21, present volume). The tragedy of Dostoevsky, like all true tragedy, involves purification and release, which can liberate the spirit and produce great joy, and this joy is associated with faith in Christ, whose tragedy purifies and saves us. Dostoevsky was not "a pessimistic and despairing writer; there is always light in his darkness, and it is the light of Christ. . . . The image of man is restored through the God-man" (p. 31, present volume).

According to Berdyaev, Dostoevsky had a single, overarching theme: man and man's destiny. "The riddle of the universe lies within man, and to solve the question of man is to solve the question of God" (p. 39 present volume). The solution to human destiny was to be found in Jesus Christ, the God-Man. Dostoevsky was a great Christian writer who denounced humanism because it was powerless to find a solution to the tragedy of human destiny. Accordingly, the work of Dostoevsky knows nothing outside of man; people, their temperament, way of living, feelings, thoughts, were his sole preoccupation. For Dostoevsky, only the human spirit exists. Berdyaev calls Dostoevsky an anthropologist, an experimenter in human nature: in his books he subjected man to spiritual experiments, putting him into extraordinary situations and then taking away all external supports one after another until his social framework had disappeared. He then explored what man would do, what path he would choose, in this terrible freedom. "Without freedom there is no man, and Dostoevsky conducted all his dialectic on man and his destiny as the dialectic of the destiny of freedom. Now the way of freedom is the way of suffering, and man must follow it to the end" (p. 66 present volume).

Berdyaev discusses Dostoevsky's conception of freedom at length, asserting that freedom is at the center of his conception of the world. For Dostoevsky, freedom is the tragic destiny of mankind and of God; it appertains to the very heart of being as a fundamental mystery. Freedom is bound up with what Berdyaev calls Dostoevsky's paradoxical theodicy: "The existence of evil is a proof of the existence of God. If the world consisted wholly and uniquely of goodness and righteousness, there would be no need for God, for the world itself would be god. God exists because evil exists. And that means that God exists because freedom exists" (p. 87, present volume).

Freedom also includes political freedom, and Dostoevsky certainly did not ignore the latter, but considered it in all its profundity (indeed, he experienced its consequences "on his own skin," as Russians say, during his years as a revolutionary, with his consequent arrest and imprisonment). According to Berdyaev, Dostoevsky's gift of spiritual vision included an ability to discern the true nature of political and social events; it can even be called a gift of political prophecy. In the most exact sense of the word, Dostoevsky was the prophet of the Russian Revolution: he revealed its inner dialectic, grasping its nature in the depth of the evolution of the spirit and not from the outward circumstances that composed the empirical reality around him. Berdyaev points out, however, that Dostoevsky's view of revolution involved an antinomy: "No one has denounced more strongly than he the falsehood and unrighteousness that make revolutions; he saw in them a mighty spirit of the Antichrist, the ambition to make a god of man. But he must not be regarded as a conservative or reactionary in the current sense: he was revolutionary-minded in a deeper way. . . . His mind was too apocalyptic to imagine any . . . restoration of a former tranquility" (pp. 134–35, present volume).

Dostoevsky's complex view of revolution is reflected in the words of Zosima, the saintly elder of *The Brothers Karamazov*: "they [revolutionaries] have more imaginative fancies than we. They aim at organizing justly, but they have rejected Christ and will end by flooding the earth with blood, for blood cries for blood and he who takes the sword shall perish by it. Were it not for Christ's covenant, men would destroy one another down to the last pair" (pp. 149–50, present volume)

But if men do succeed in destroying one another, it will be because of their freedom (something sacred for both Dostoevsky and Berdyaev), and the Grand Inquisitor has a solution: take men's freedom away from them. In *The Brothers Karamazov*, Ivan relates to Alyosha a parable he has written: "The Legend of the Grand Inquisitor." In this parable, Christ returns to earth in Seville at the time of the Inquisition. He performs a number of miracles. The people recognize him and adore him, but he is arrested by Inquisition leaders and sentenced to be burned to death the next day. The Grand Inquisitor visits him in his cell and denounces him, explaining to him how he, the Inquisitor, has succeeded in helping men, whereas he, Christ, has failed. The Inquisitor frames his denunciation of Jesus around the three questions Satan asked Jesus during the temptation in the desert. These are the temptation to turn stones into bread, the temptation to cast Himself from the Temple and be saved by the angels, and the temptation to rule over all the kingdoms of the world. The Inquisitor asserts that Christ rejected these three temptations in favor of freedom. For Berdyaev "The Legend of the Grand Inquisitor" is the high point of Dostoevsky's work and the crown of his dialectic, in which he solves the radical problem, that of human freedom. "Every man is offered the alternatives of the Grand Inquisitor or of Christ, and he must accept one or the other. . . . In the Grand

Inquisitor's system, self-will leads to the negation and loss of freedom of spirit, which can be found again in Christ alone" (pp. 188–89, present volume).

For Berdyaev, two universal principles confront one another in the Legend: freedom and compulsion, belief in the meaning of life and disbelief, divine love and humanitarian pity, Christ and Antichrist. Freedom, the Inquisitor argues, is incompatible with happiness and should appertain only to a tiny aristocracy, and he accuses Christ of acting as if he did not love man when he imposed freedom on all men. If man is to be happy, his conscience must be lulled, and that can be most easily done by taking away his freedom of choice. The Grand Inquisitor promises that men shall be saved from "the great anxiety and terrible agony they endure at present in making a free decision for themselves. And all these millions and millions of creatures will be happy. . . ." (pp. 194–95, present volume). Christ has honored men too much by offering them freedom: they are too savage to accept freedom or even to acknowledge God's call to them. As Ivan Karamazov says: "The astonishing thing is that this notion of the necessity of God has been able to get a footing in the mind of so savage and vicious an animal as man, so holy and moving and wise is it, and so honoring to the individual" (p. 195, present volume).

Christ refused the three temptations in the name of man's spiritual freedom, since it was not his will that the human spirit should be won over by bread, by an earthly kingdom, or by miracles. The Grand Inquisitor, on the contrary, welcomes these temptations in the name of human happiness and contentment, and in welcoming them he renounces freedom. This is what he tells Christ: "It was in thy power to have taught men all that they want to know on this earth, that is, to whom they must look up, to whom and how they can hand over their conscience, and how they can all join together and make a single unanimous common ant-heap of themselves, since the craving for a universal fusion is the third and last torment of man." (p. 196, present volume).

In summing up, let us remember Berdyaev's words that the existence of Dostoevsky is by itself "sufficient justification for the existence of the Russian people in the world." Berdyaev issues a warning, however: Even though we are Dostoevsky's spiritual heirs, he does not teach us how to live: there are dangers in his spiritual truths and to draw a life-lesson from them is a perilous experience. For Dostoevsky, man's only road is though tragedy, inner division, the attainment of light through darkness; and his greatness lay in the fact that he showed the light shining in the darkness. But Berdyaev notes that, unfortunately, "the Russian is inclined to jump into the dark waters and . . . seems unable to defend himself against the destructive attacks of dionysiac passions. Dostoevsky portrayed the Russian entangled in the elementary activities of the soul, and he found out important things about the Russian's spirit and the human spirit at large; but he never set forth spiritual maturity, the spirit controlling the chaotic movements of the soul and directing it to higher ends" (pp. 221–22, present volume). But even though Dostoevsky takes us into very dark places, he does not let darkness have the last word: his books do not leave us with an impression of somber and despairing pessimism, for with the darkness there comes a great light: "Christ is victorious over the world and illuminates all things" (p. 225, present volume).

BORIS JAKIM
2008

TRANSLATOR'S NOTE

NICHOLAS ALEXANDROVITCH BERDYAEV was born at Kiev, the "God-protected mother of Russian cities," in 1874 and published his first book, *Subjectivism and Individualism in Social Philosophy*, at the age of twenty-six, since when he has become one of the most prolific and widely read of contemporary Russian writers. He suffered exile for a time during youth and was again threatened with banishment just before the fall of the imperial government: this was for having criticized the erastianism of the Governing Synod of the Orthodox Church in his country. After the revolution he received the chair of philosophy in the University of Moscow, but after two terms of imprisonment was expelled by the Bolshevists in 1922 as an upholder of religion. M. Berdyaev now lives in Paris, where he directs the Academy of the Philosophy of Religion, which he founded in Germany, and edits a review called *Putj* ("The Way").

The writings of M. Berdyaev are already appreciated by many English-speaking readers, and he is specially qualified to expound the mind of Dostoievsky, not least because both (and Soloviev, too) had a common spiritual father in Nicholas Federov, whose influence on Russian thought has only lately begun to be understood. This translation of *Mirosozertzanie Dostoievskago* has been made from the French version of Lucienne Julien Cain, *L'Esprit de Dostoievski*, published by Editions Saint Michel in Paris. The French version has modifications of the Russian text which M. Berdyaev wished to be taken into account. The titles of the novels are given according to the translations of Constance Garnett.

D. A.

FOREWORD

DOSTOIEVSKY has played a decisive part in my
spiritual life. While I was still a youth a slip from
him, so to say, was grafted upon me. He stirred and
lifted up my soul more than any other writer or
philosopher has done, and for me people are always
divided into "dostoievskyites" and those to whom
his spirit is foreign. It is undoubtedly due to his
"cursed questioning" that philosophical problems
were present to my consciousness at so early an age,
and some new aspect of him is revealed to me every
time I read him. The *Legend of the Grand Inquisitor*, in
particular, made such an impression on my young
mind that when I turned to Jesus Christ for the first
time I saw him under the appearance that he bears
in the Legend.

At the base of my notion of the world as I see it
there has always lain the idea of liberty, and in this
fundamental intuition of liberty I found Dostoievsky
as it were on his own special ground. Accordingly, I
long wanted to devote a book to him but was able to
realize my wish only to the extent of a few articles.
Finally, the lectures which I delivered on him at the
seminar I directed during the winter of 1920-21
determined me to bring together my thoughts on the

7

subject, and so this book came to be written. In it I have not only tried to display Dostoievsky's own conception of the world, but also to set down a considerable part of what constitutes my own.

N. A. B.

CHAPTER I

SPIRIT

I AM not setting out here to write an essay in the
history of literature or to make a biography or likeness of Fyodor Dostoievsky; still less is this to be a
book of literary criticism. Nor, on the other hand,
can it be said that I tackle my subject from the psychological angle, that my intention is to draw conclusions in the psychological order. No; the task I
have set myself is something quite different. My aim
is to display Dostoievsky's spiritual side; I want to
explore in all its depth the way in which he apprehended the universe and intuitively to reconstruct
out of these elements his whole "world-vision."

For Dostoievsky was a great thinker and a great
visionary as well as a great artist, a dialectician of
genius and Russia's greatest metaphysician. Ideas
play a preponderating part in his work, and his
dialectic has as big a place in it as his remarkable
psychology. This dialectic is of the very essence of
his art: by art he reaches to the bases of the world of
ideas, and the world of ideas in its turn makes his
art fruitful. For him ideas live with an organic life,
they have a living and ineluctable destiny; their

existence is highly dynamic: there is nothing static about them, no standing still, no hardening. Dostoievsky kept his attention exclusively on the living process of this dynamism, stirring up ideas in his work that are like whirlpools of fire. He was not interested in tepid notions. There was a dash of the spirit of Heraclitus in him: everything is heat and motion, opposition and struggle. For Dostoievsky ideas are fiery billows, never frozen categories; they are bound up with the destiny of man, of the world, of God himself. They determine those destinies. They are ontological; that is to say, comprise within themselves the very substance of being, and conceal a latent energy as destructive as dynamite—Dostoievsky shows how their explosion spreads ruin all around. But they have life-giving energy as well. The world of ideas conceived by Dostoievsky is entirely original and has nothing in common with that of Plato. Ideas are not prototypes of being, primary entities, much less norms; they are the destiny of living being, its burning motive-power. Dostoievsky no less than Plato recognized that ideas as such have a value of their own; and, in spite of the present tendency to deny this autonomous value and to be blind to their worth in any writer, Dostoievsky cannot be understood—indeed, his books had better be left alone—unless the reader is prepared to be immersed in a vast strange universe of ideas. Dostoievsky's work is a veritable "feast of thought," and those who will not sit down to table, because their sceptical minds deny the usefulness of all thought, are self-condemned to a diminution and dulling of their own spiritual experience.

Dostoievsky shows us new worlds, worlds in motion, by which alone human destinies can be made intelligible. The way into them cannot be found so long as one's enquiries are confined to psychology or to the formal aspect of art, and it is precisely this universe that I want to enter and explore in order to seize what I will call Dostoievsky's *conception of the world*. What exactly is a writer's conception of the world if it is not his intuitive penetration into its innermost essence, what he discovers in life and the universe? So far as Dostoievsky is concerned there is no question of an abstract system— which indeed is not to be expected from an artist— but of an intuition of genius about human and universal destiny. An intuition that is artistic, not exclusively so, but intellectual and philosophical as well, a true *gnosis*: for in a special sense of the word Dostoievsky was a gnostic; his work is a system of knowing, a science of the spirit. His conception of the world was in the highest degree dynamic, and we must look at it in that way; the internal contradictions of his work will then vanish, and it will verify the principle of *coincidentia oppositorum*.

A great deal has been written about Dostoievsky, much of it true and interesting, but nobody has succeeded in compassing his personality wholly and completely. Those who have set out to do so have observed only an incomplete aspect of their subject, for their studies were restricted to some particular feature which alone corresponded to their special line of research. Accordingly, Dostoievsky is for some a champion of the "downtrodden and oppressed"; for others, a ruthless genius; for yet others, the prophet of a new Christianity; he is the discoverer of the "man from the underworld", the typical representative of Eastern Orthodoxy, the herald of the Russian messianic idea. Nobody has attempted a synthesis of these diverse aspects, least of all the traditional school of Russian criticism, whose exponents are as blind to Dostoievsky as they are to all the other great phenomena of our national literature. Mikhailovsky,* for example, was constitutionally incapable of understanding him. The fact is that really to "get inside" Dostoievsky it is necessary to have a certain sort of soul—one in some way akin to his own—and we had to wait for the spiritual and intellectual movement which marked the beginning of the twentieth century before such souls could be found. The extraordinary interest in Dostoievsky and his work dates from this time.

Special mention must be made of Merejkovsky's

---

* Nicholas Mikhailovsky (1842-1904). A "populist" leader who exercised an almost unlimited influence over the radical *intelligentzia* of Russia for nearly twenty years. TR.

book, *Lev Tolstoy i Dostoievski* ("Leo Tolstoy and Dostoievsky"), the best one so far. The author's defect is in being too exclusively preoccupied with Dostoievsky's religious theories, which he sets out parallel with Tolstoy's. For Merejkovsky, Dostoievsky was only the instrument of spreading the religion of the resurrection of the body, and he failed to appreciate the unique originality of the spirit that was behind it; therefore, though he opened some hitherto unknown windows on his subject, his book is fundamentally misleading. A great writer is a complete manifestation of the spirit, and as such he ought to be dealt with as a unified whole. This unity can be apprehended only intuitively, by identifying oneself with it and "living" it oneself. It is no good analysing it from outside with the intention of piecing it together afterwards, for it will have died under the vivisector's knife. A man of genius is a high spiritual phenomenon which one must approach with a believing soul. We are not going to imitate so many of our contemporaries, who are inclined always to suspect as it were a hidden disease in a writer whom they love and so treat of him scalpel in hand: we will come to Dostoievsky by the believers' road, plunging straightforwardly into the whirlpool of his dynamic ideas that we may attain the secret of his fundamental conception of the world.

It has been said that all genius is national, even, nay, the more, when it is most human. This is incontestably true of Dostoievsky. He was specifically Russian, Russian right through, the most Russian of all Russian writers: at the same time he was the most human, both in himself and in those of whom he wrote. "I have always been a real Russian," he wrote to Maikov, and his work is a Russian interpretation of the Universal. That is why it arouses so much interest among Westerners: they look to him both for a general revelation about the problems which beset them and a particular revelation about that strange puzzling thing, the Russian world of the East. He who understands Dostoievsky integrally has assimilated an essential part of the Russian soul and has read in part the mystery of Russia.

Another of her great geniuses, Tiutshev,* has said that "It takes more than intelligence to understand Russia, and she cannot be measured with a two-foot rule." Dostoievsky reflects all those contradictions and antinomies of the Russian mind that have called forth so many contradictory judgments of the country and its people; in him its spiritual architecture can be seen and studied. Russians classify themselves as "apocalypsists" and "nihilists," showing thereby that they are not comfortable in a temperate

* The "poet of elemental night." He wrote strictly according to eighteenth-century ideas of classicism, and is accounted by some Russia's second greatest poet. TR.

psychical climate, their constitution driving them irresistibly towards extremes; the same tendency to excess, the same desire to push things to their logical conclusion, force them to these opposite poles of looking for the revelation of a new heaven and earth and of nihilism. Thus the structure of the Russian soul differs profoundly from that of a German, who is a mystic or a "criticist," or that of a Frenchman, who is a sceptic or a dogmatist. The Russian is the most unfitted of all Europeans to elaborate a culture and to trace a consistent historical path. Can such a people ever be happy as a people? From the opposed sides whence they are come, excess of religion as well as of atheism, apocalypsism and nihilism are equally destructive of culture and history that occupy a middle way. Russia has rebelled against this culture and this history, she is suppressing all their values and making a clean slate, but it is difficult to decide whether she is doing so as a nihilist or as an apocalypsist who believes that the world is going to be overwhelmed by a huge religious catastrophe. "Nihilism has appeared among us because we are all nihilists," wrote Dostoievsky in his diary, and it is this nihilism that he probed to the bottom, a nihilism, I repeat, that is only an inverted apocalypsism.

It can be seen at once how such a disposition of soul impedes the historical path of a people and the elaboration of cultural values, how unfavourable it is

to all spiritual discipline. That was what Leontiev*
meant when he said that a Russian can be a saint
but not a "worthy fellow." "Worthiness" is a sort
of moral compromise, a middle-class virtue that
doesn't appeal to extremists who are sure that the
end of the world is at hand. This characteristic of
extremeness has been disastrous to the Russian
people, for saints are exceptions among them and the
greater number is given up to unrighteousness; a
few attain a spiritual life of the highest order, the
rest remain below the average of other peoples: that
is why there is such a striking contrast between the
Russian spiritual *élite* and the unlettered mob.
There is no general culture in Russia, no cultured
society, and almost no cultural tradition.   In this
matter nearly all Russians are nihilists.   Why?
Because culture does not resolve any ultimate problems beyond our earthly economy; on the contrary, it strengthens the human sphere.   For the
"Russian boy" (a favourite expression of Dostoiev-
ky), absorbed in the solution of metaphysical questions, God, immortality, or in the organization of
mankind on a new model, as well as for any atheist,
socialist, or anarchist, culture is an obstacle in the
way of their impetuous rush towards a consumma-
tion.   Where Western man strives to organize the

* An advocate in theory of extreme conservatism and aristocracy.
He began his career in diplomacy and died a monk of the Troitza
monastery near Moscow (1891). Tr.

world historically, the Russians want to attain a definitive result at once, in one big jump. Hence their dislike for the formal element in law, in sovereignty, in art, in philosophy, in religion, for it involves measure and sets up boundaries which are precisely what the nihilist and apocalypsist reject in their revolt. Spengler writes in his interesting book called *Preussentum und Sozialismus* ("Prussia and Socialism"), that Russia is a world apart, mysterious and unintelligible to the European, and he sees in her an "apocalyptic rebellion against antiquity."

The Russian nihilists and apocalypsists are at the extreme poles of the soul. Dostoievsky analyses this double tendency to the very bottom, and was the first to denounce that sort of metaphysical hysteria of the Russian, his excessive inclination towards obsession and magic. He studied the Russian revolutionary proclivities, so clearly related to the reactionary elements, to the *chernosotenstvo* ("Blackhundred"),* as it was called in those days. The subsequent fate of Russia has justified his prophecy: the revolution was, to a considerable extent, "according to Dostoievsky." However destructive and murderous it has been, it is none the less Russian and national: self-wastage and self-destruction are national characteristics of Russia.

* From *chernaya sotnia*, "black hundred," an extreme reactionary organization advocating a policy of *pogroms* against the liberal *intelligentzia* and the Jews, and responsible for many disturbances and crimes. TR.

Dostoievsky, enormously helped by these racial dispositions, transcended the limits of psychic life and revealed the spiritual depths and distances that lie beyond. He uncovered a volcanic crater in every being, under the layers that psychologists had explored and illumined by the light of reason and brought under rational norms—and the eruption of those underground volcanoes fills Dostoievsky's work. It takes a long time for this latent force to collect its revolutionary spiritual energy; the enclosing earth becomes more and more volcanic, while on the surface the soul keeps its old equilibrium in submission to ancient laws: then suddenly there is an explosion as of dynamite. Dostoievsky was the herald of the spirit of revolution on its way to accomplishment; he expresses nothing in his work but the impassioned and tumultuous dynamism of human nature. Man in that mood tears himself away from the social order, stops obeying the rules, and enters a universe in another dimension. For with Dostoievsky a new soul and a new perception of the world were born; and he carried this exclusive dynamism of the spirit, this flame-like mobility, within himself. "The worst thing of all," he wrote to Maikov, "is that my nature is too passionate and unrestrained. I always go to extremes; I have exceeded the limit all my life." His interior passion ate up his soul with voracious fire, fire from the underworld from which he had to escape to arrive at the light of day. All Dostoievsky's heroes arc really himself: they tread the path that he trod; the different aspects of his being, his difficulties, his restlessness, his bitter experience are all theirs. That is why there is no epic quality about his work, no objective picture of objective life, no re-creation of the exterior world in its diversity, nothing, in a word, of that which constitutes the most powerful part of the work of Leo Tolstoy. Dostoievsky's novels are not, properly speaking, novels at all; they are parts of a tragedy, the inner tragedy of human destiny, the unique human spirit revealing itself in its various aspects and at different stages of its journey.

It was a gift of Dostoievsky to be able to grasp and present man in all his passionate excited activity, and the reader himself is carried along by the hurricane. These upheavals are hidden in the depth of man's being; Dostoievsky's art was to express these underground disturbances of human nature, whose dynamic pressure continually throws existing things into confusion. It is no use looking to any established order sanctioned by past history (as Tolstoy did); man's eyes must be turned towards the unknown future, the Becoming. Such art is prophetic: it unveils the secret of man, and for that purpose studies him in his unconsciousness, folly, and wickedness rather than in his stable surroundings, the normal and rational forms of his everyday social life. For the deeps of human nature are sounded not in sanity but in insanity, not in law-abidingness but in criminality, in obscure unconscious tendencies and not in daily life and in the parts of the soul that have been enlightened by the daylight of consciousness. Dostoievsky's work is in a very high degree dionysiac, and Dionysism gives birth to tragedy, for it shows us man's nature only in a state of exaltation, and after such pictures everything seems savourless and flat: it is like coming back to our own three-dimensional organized world after visiting another and different universe. A careful reading of Dostoievsky is an event in life from which the soul receives a baptism of fire. The man who has lived for a time in Dostoievsky's world has seen as it were "unpublished forms" of being, for he is above all a great revolutionary of the spirit opposing himself to every kind of stagnation and hardening.

There is a marked contrast between Dostoievsky and Tolstoy. Dostoievsky, forerunner of the revolutionary spirit on its way to realization, his tremendously dynamic nature directed towards Becoming, is the one who loves his native soil, who affirms the goodness of historical tradition and of things handed down as sacred, who recognizes the government and the official church of Russia. Tolstoy, on the other hand, who was never a spiritual revolutionary but a portrayer of static things, of the social organization as it existed and as it exists, who looked backward to

the past, who was in no sense a prophet, Tolstoy it
was who rebelled against all historical and religious
traditions, who with unprecedented intransigence
denied Orthodoxy and flouted the Empire, who
would not even accept the primacy of culture. Dostoievsky showed the profound nature of Russian
nihilism; Tolstoy declared himself a nihilist, a de-
stroyer of sacred relics and of all values. Dostoievsky
knew that revolution was brewing underground in
man's spirit and that it would surely come: he foresaw its methods and its results. Tolstoy knew nothing about a revolution, foresaw nothing, yet himself
was caught up like a blind man in the machinery of
the revolutionary process. Dostoievsky kept to the
spiritual plane, from whence he saw everything;
Tolstoy stuck to the psychic and bodily domain, and
could not see what was going on under the surface.
It is possible that Tolstoy was a finer artist than
Dostoievsky, that his novels, as novels, are the better;
he is an accomplished painter of that which is, while
Dostoievsky is concerned only with that which is to
be, and perfection is easier of attainment upon
static material than upon material in motion. But
Dostoievsky is the greater thinker of the two, his
awareness of things is more extensive, and he knows
the eternal human contradiction which makes it
necessary to take one step back for every two forward, while Tolstoy went straight on without turning
his head. Again, Dostoievsky saw life with reference

to the spirit of man: that is why he knew that the revolution seething within that spirit would take place; but for Tolstoy life is just an emanation of nature, merely the fluid that continually vitalizes plants and animals; he could see only a biological process, against whose laws he rebelled. And his one-sided morality could in no case have been shared by such a seer of the human heart as Dostoievsky. We can conclude that, if Tolstoy brought to the portrayal of the forms of the past a perfection of art which Dostoievsky could not compass for his more elusive material of the future, then the art of the one is the art of Apollo and of the other the art of Dionysos.

The parallelism between the two is curious under another head. All his life Tolstoy was seeking God as a pagan seeks God; his mind was obsessed by theology, and he was a bad theologian. Dostoievsky, on the other hand, was much less concerned with God than with man and his destiny, with the riddle of the spirit; he was not haunted by theology but by anthropology; he did not have to solve the divine problem as does the pagan, but the problem of mankind, which is the problem of the spiritual man, the Christian. Man is confronted by the question of God, God is confronted by the question of man, and it is probably precisely by way of the human riddle that we can best approach him. Dostoievsky was not a theologian, but for all that he was nearer than

Tolstoy to the living God, who revealed himself to
him in man's destiny—perhaps it is more expedient
to be an anthropologist than a theologian!

Was Dostoievsky a realist? Before this question
can be answered it must be decided in what measure
great art can be realistic. It is true that Dostoievsky
liked to call himself so, and regarded his realism as
being the very realism of life itself. But he certainly
did not use the word in the sense given to it by official
critics when they affirm the existence of a "realistic
school" whose head is Gogol: nothing that they
intend to cover by that label is to be found in Dostoievsky (or in Gogol, for that matter). The truth is
that all essential art is symbolical: it is a bridge
built between two worlds, a sign that expresses a
deep, authentic reality; the end of art surpasses
experimental reality and is to express hidden reality,
not in a direct way but by means of projected
shadows. Now nobody was less preoccupied with
the empirical world than Dostoievsky; his art is completely immersed in the profound realities of the
spiritual universe. Even the construction of his books
in no way resembles that of the so-called realistic
novels. Throughout his exterior plots, relating some
improbable tale of crime, we feel the presence of
this inner reality, something different, more real
than the others. For Dostoievsky, the ultimate
realities are not the external forms of life, flesh and
blood men, but their inner depths, the destiny of the

human spirit. Reality is the relations of man with God and with Satan, reality is the ideas by which man lives.

That cleavage (*dédoublement*) in the spirit which is the essential theme of all Dostoievsky's novels does not lend itself to realistic treatment. The marvellous picture of the relations between Ivan Karamazov and Smerdyakov by which the internal division (*dédoublement*) in Ivan is made clear cannot be called realistic, and still less that of the relations between him and the Evil One. Nor can Dostoievsky be made a realistic psychologist—he was not a psychologist but a "pneumatologist," a symbolistic metaphysician. Beneath conscious life there was always hidden an unconscious world with which his visionary expectations were in touch, and he saw that human beings reach out to one another not only along the visible threads of consciousness but even more along the mysterious lines whose roots are hidden in the depths of their unconscious life: such are the invisible bonds which join Muishkin to Nastasia Philippovna and to Rogojin, Raskolnikov to Svidrigailov, Ivan Karamazov to Smerdyakov, Stavroguin to the Khromonojka and to Shatov. They are bound together by links that are not of this world's forging; there is nothing contingent in their relationship, no place for the accidents of an empirical realism: it seems as though the meeting of these beings were ordained from all eternity by a higher will, that they are branded with the mark of a fate that must be fulfilled. Their collisions and reciprocal reactions do not express any deceiving objective reality but that hidden reality, the inner destiny of humankind. In them is truly expressed the great "idea" of the universe which answers the riddle of man and of the road which he treads. All this is very unlike the contents of what is commonly called a "realistic novel." Nevertheless, though it is absolutely wrong to call Dostoievsky a "realist," we may say that he is a mystical-realist.

Literary historians and critics, always keen on finding reciprocal borrowings and influences among authors, have not failed to name affinities for Dostoievsky, especially in his earlier period, notably Victor Hugo, George Sand, Dickens, and even Hoffman. However, his only obvious literary relationship is with one of the greatest Western writers, who was as little of a realist as he was himself, namely, Balzac; as for his fellow Russians, Gogol had some influence on the early novels, but the two treat human nature in quite different ways. Gogol saw man's face in a process of dissolution and pictured it only as a grimacing simian mask: the art of Andrew Biely is the nearest to his. But for Dostoievsky human personality is inalienable, and he finds it even in the most degraded specimens of mankind. For the rest, from the moment that he really found himself and advanced his new principle, Dostoievsky was beyond

all outside influence and borrowing: his was a creative manifestation almost without precedent in the
world's history. *Letters from the Underworld (Zapiski
iz podpolya)** is the mark of division between his two
periods. Up to that time he had been only a psychologist (though an inventive one) and a humanitarian, full of compassion for the "poor folk," for
the "downtrodden and oppressed," for the heroes of
The House of the Dead. Letters from the Underworld
inaugurated Dostoievsky's superb dialectic. From
being only a psychologist he becomes a metaphysician, following the tragedy of the human spirit to
its very end; he ceases to be a humanitarian on the
old pattern and no longer has anything in common
with Hugo or Sand or Dickens; he breaks definitively
with the theories of Bielinsky.† If he still loves and
pities mankind his love has something new and
tragic about it. Man more than ever holds the
centre of the stage of his work, human destiny is the
only thing that interests him; he is no longer treated
as a superficial creature but is followed into his newly
discovered spiritual depths: a new human kingdom
has arisen, a "dostoievskian" kingdom. Dostoievsky
is a writer of tragedy; in him the unrest that is
latent in all Russian literature reaches its state of

* Translated into English by C. J. Hogarth, London, 1913. TR.

† Vissarion Bielinsky (1811-1848). A leader among the Westernizers who, beginning as a romantic idealist, became the "spiritual
father of Russian radicalism." TR.

highest tension: the wound dealt by the sorrowful
destiny of man and his world is quick in him.

Here it must be recalled in parenthesis that the
Russians have never had a "renaissance"; an
unhappy fate has withheld from them this good for-
tune of other peoples. Possibly they saw the flush of
a comparable dawn at the beginning of the nineteenth century, in the time of Alexander I—the
highest point of their culture—when poetry blos-
somed with a freedom that spread a kind of exulta-
tion. But it was a delight in a happy creation that
was soon extinguished; even during Pushkin's life-
time it was already poisoned. Russian literature in
the nineteenth century did not follow Pushkin;
it was consumed in pain and distress, suffering for
the salvation of the world as though it were expiating
some sin. The dark figure of the tragically afflicted
Tshaadaev* stands at the beginning of the movement
in which thought in nineteenth-century Russia came
to maturity; Lermontov,† Gogol, Tiutshev wrote
not in the spirit of the Renaissance but in torment
and anxiety. After them, on the other hand, there
was the strange apparition of Constantine Leontiev,
who seemed like a man of the sixteenth century from

* A remarkable thinker (d. 1856) who was in many ways the forerunner of Soloviev. His works were published by Father J. Gagarin,
S.J., in Paris in 1862. TR.

† Michael Lermontov was of Scots descent and one of the best of
the Russian romantic poets. He was killed by a friend in a duel about
a woman in 1841 when he was twenty-seven years of age. TR.

western Europe who had strayed into this hostile and grief-stricken Russia of the nineteenth. Then were seen the topmost peaks of our literature, Tolstoy and Dostoievsky. There is nothing reminiscent of the Renaissance about them. They are in the throes of religious anguish, they seek salvation—that is the characteristic of Russian creative writers, they seek salvation, thirst to make expiation, they suffer for the world.

The work of Dostoievsky is the climax of Russian literature and it is the finest expression of its earnest, religious, tormented character; its path of sorrow led to Dostoievsky, and all the shadows of Russian life and history were gathered together in him. But there was a glimmer of light, shining through a crack in the old world. The tragedy of Dostoievsky, like all true tragedy, involves purification and release, though those who are held by it in unescapable darkness, who accept only its misery, do not understand this. There is freeing of the spirit and joy to be had from reading Dostoievsky, the joy that one gets from suffering. It is the path the Christian has to tread. Dostoievsky renewed faith in man and in the notion of his depths, which Humanism had not recognized. Humanism destroys man, but he is born again if he believes in God—and only on this condition can he believe in himself. Dostoievsky does not disassociate faith in man from faith in Christ, the God-man. Throughout his life he had kept a special

reverence, a sort of mystical love, for that divine
face, and it was in Christ's name and for love of him
that he gave up that humanitarian circle whose
prophet was Bielinsky. This faith of his Dostoievsky
tested in the crucible of his doubts and tempered
with their fire. He wrote in one of his notebooks:
"No other expression of atheism has ever had such
force in Europe [as humanitarianism]. It was not as
a child that I learnt to believe in Christ and confess
his faith. My Hosanna has burst forth from a huge
furnace of doubt." He had then lost his youthful
belief in Schillerism, by which name he designated
the cult of the "great and beautiful"—idealistic
humanitarianism. In his experience Schillerism had
not survived a single test, while his faith in Christ
had stood up to them all; so he gave up the humanitarian belief in man and believed in him in the
Christian way, deepening and strengthening that
faith. For that very reason Dostoievsky could not be
a pessimistic and despairing writer; there is always
light in his darkness, and it is the light of Christ. It is
indeed true that he shows man wandering among the
chasms of inner division (it is a fundamental theme
in his work), but this division does not in the end
destroy the identity of the individual person. The
image of man is restored through the God-man.

Dostoievsky belonged to that race of writers to
whom it is given to express *themselves* in their work;

he gave voice to all the doubts and contradictions of his own mind, and perhaps it is because he hid nothing of what was going on in himself that he was able to find out such astonishing things about mankind in general. The destiny of his characters is his own, their doubts and dualities are his, their iniquities are the sins hidden in his own soul. The story of Dostoievsky's life is therefore much less interesting than his writings, his letters tell us less than his novels; in his fiction he strips himself bare, and thanks to this confession he is much less of a puzzle than many other writers, Gogol, for example, who is a most mysterious figure among Russian authors: nothing can be learned about himself from his books and his secret seems to have died with him. It is the same with the philosopher Vladimir Soloviev in our own day; in the whole of his philosophical and theological treatises there is no sign of his personal trials and difficulties; only in his poetry does an occasional more intimate note make itself heard. The nature of Dostoievsky's genius, on the other hand, was such that in the exploration and analysis of his own life he showed at the same time the universal destiny of man. He hides from us nothing of his contrary ideals, from the Evil and Sodom to our Lady and the Good: man torn between the two was one of his great themes. Even his epilepsy was something more to him than just an accidental malady.

Dostoievsky called himself an "aboriginal" and

his ideology was exclusively that of his race; he never severed the roots that bound him to his native soil. Nevertheless, it would be a mistake to number him among the Slavophils; he belongs to another age. Set beside them, he is a vagabond, a Russian strayed into the realm of the spirit; he has neither lands nor mansion nor even the cosy quarters of some small country manor-house; he is bound to no stable form of living—everything about him is dynamic, restless, breathing revolution. He was a man of the Apocalypse, and the Slavophils were never touched by the apocalyptical complaint. Dostoievsky above all embodied the way of the wanderer and the rebel, which he judged to be highly characteristic of his people; the Slavophils on the contrary were rooted in the earth upon which they had been born and bred, and drew their strength from it: it seemed firm as rock beneath their feet, while Dostoievsky was the man of underground convulsions—his element was fire and his mark was movement. His views differed from theirs in everything: they were opposed to Western influence, he was a partizan of Europe, they championed the old Moscow, he admired the era of Peter the Great and upheld Petersburg. We shall see later how he differed from them in his ideas on Russia in general; all I want to show now is that Dostoievsky was not in any sense a Slavophil. What he did represent, and represented exactly, was the writers of his country, the men who

c—d

live only by their pens. Apart from literature he
made nothing; he lived on his work spiritually and
materially, and his sad history accurately sums up
the destiny of the writers of Russia.

Dostoievsky was among the most brilliant and
keen-minded men of all time. His intelligence was
extraordinary, and probably exceeded even his skill
as an artist. Herein he differed from Tolstoy, who
was a greater artist than he was a thinker: his ideas
are sometimes astonishingly shallow, almost commonplace. But for sheer intelligence there is no one
to compare with Dostoievsky unless it be that great
light of the Renaissance, Shakespeare. Even the
mind of Goethe, great among the greatest, had not
the same keenness and dialectical profundity. This
is all the more surprising since Dostoievsky lived in a
frantically dionysiac atmosphere not at all con-
ducive to clear thinking. But for him this delirious
excitement, so far from inhibiting thought, fulfilled
it, in such a way that ideas and their dialectic follow a
dionysiac rhythm. Dostoievsky is drunk with ideas,
for in his books ideas intoxicate, but in the midst of
it all the fine edge of his intelligence is never blunted.
This is certainly impossible of understanding by
those who are not interested in the dialectic of the
impressive progress of Dostoievsky's thought, who see
in him no more than an artist or a psychologist, for
all his work is a solution of a vast problem of ideas.

The hero of the *Letters from the Underworld* is an idea, Raskolnikov is an idea, Stavroguin is an idea, Kirilov, Shatov, Verhovensky, Ivan Karamazov—ideas; all these people are as it were submerged by ideas, drunk with them. They only open their mouths to develop their ideological dialectic; everything revolves around "these cursed everlasting questions." This does not mean that Dostoievsky's novels are dissertations for the propagation of such-and-such a particular theory. Actually, ideas are imminent in his writing and are brought out in a purely artistic way; he is an "idealist" writer, idealist not as that word is understood in common speech, but in its platonic sense. He conceived new and fundamental notions, but they were always conceived in motion, dynamic.

Dostoievsky wrote modestly of himself, "I am rather weak in philosophy—but not in my love for philosophy, which is very strong." He was weak enough in the academical philosophy which suited him so ill, but his intuitive genius knew the right paths and he was in fact a true philosopher, the greatest Russia has known. He gave a great deal to philosophy (the philosophy of anthropology, of history, of religion, of morality, all owe him much), and philosophical speculation ought to make a lot of use of his conceptions. He may have learnt but little from philosophy, but he taught it much; he may have left only provisional questions to it, but where ultimate things are concerned it is philosophy which for long years has lived under the banner of Dostoievsky.

Dostoievsky unveiled a new spiritual world: he restored to man the spiritual depth of which he had been bereft when it was removed to the inaccessible heights of a transcendent plane. Man had been left with only his bodily envelope and the lesser faculties of his soul; he could no longer see the dimension of depth. The Orthodox Church began this deprivation when she relegated spiritual life to another and transcendent world and created a religion for the soul that was home-sick for the spiritual life it had lost. This process could only lead to positivism, gnosticism, and materialism, that is, to the utter despiritualization of man and his universe. The transcendent world itself was pushed back into the unknowable and all the ways leading to it were closed, till at last its very existence was denied. Thus the hostility of ecclesiastical authorities towards all gnosticism brought about an increase of agnosticism; their attempts to make spiritual profundity external to man resulted in the denial of all spiritual experience and the shutting-up of mankind in a material and psychological reality. Dostoievsky, as bearer of a great message from the spirit, was in reaction from all these tendencies. He brought back spiritual life to within man, and made him cast off the superficial realities in which he was swathed: he was to be a spiritual creature again. Dostoievsky put no limits or boundaries to experience of the spirit, the scope of its activities could be observed in the immanence of their interior movement, God could be reached in man and by man.

Such is the road of freedom which Dostoievsky put forward, and at its end is Jesus Christ, in the depths of man's soul. It can be seen at once that such a religion is in opposition to a religion of authority; it is as free as may be, and seems from outside to be permeated with the notion of liberty. In his religious conceptions Dostoievsky never attained a total unity, he failed to resolve their contradictions completely, but for all that this new free religion represented something absolute for him. Passages can be found in his *Dnevnik pisatelia** ("Diary of a Writer") which show that there were contradictions in his thought even about this; but in this "Diary" he wrote down together all the fundamental ideas which are scattered throughout his other books and are developed particularly in the novels. It is among them that the ideological dialectic of the "Legend of the Grand Inquisitor" is found, and it is precisely there that he affirms this free religion.

It cannot be repeated too often or too definitely

* Partly translated in *Pages from the Journal of an Author* by S. Koteliansky and J. Middleton Murry, London, 1916. There is a fuller translation into French in three volumes, Paris, 1927. Tr.

that (contrary to a too common opinion) the mind
of Dostoievsky tended to build rather than to pull
down, that his spirit moved him to affirmation and
not to negation. But he saw God, man, and the
world across all the agonizing confusion of inner
division and darkness. If he completely understood
the nature of Russian nihilism, he was himself anti-
nihilist (unlike Tolstoy, who caught the nihilist
fever). To-day, Dostoievsky is nearer to us than ever
before: we have moved nearer to him; and fresh
parts of his work become comprehensible in the
light of the tragic history of the Russians in our own
time.

CHAPTER II

MAN

DOSTOIEVSKY devoted the whole of his creative energy to one single theme, man and man's destiny. He was anthropological and anthropocentric to an almost inexpressible degree: the problem of man was his absorbing passion. For he did not see him as just a natural phenomenon, like any other though rather superior, but as a microcosm, the centre of being, the sun around which all else moves: the riddle of the universe is within man, and to solve the question of man is to solve the question of God. The whole of Dostoievsky's work is a plea for man, a plea which goes to the length of strife with God, which antinomy is resolved by referring human destiny to Jesus Christ, the God-man. So exclusively anthropological a conception is possible only in a Christian world and era: the ancient world can show us nothing like it; it was Christianity that turned the world towards man and made him the centre of the material universe. Dostoievsky's attitude to mankind was intensely Christian and he may be called a great Christian writer who denounced as the essential defect of Humanism its powerlessness to find a solution to the tragedy of human destiny.

Accordingly, the work of Dostoievsky knows nothing outside of man, nothing even of the things which bind him to the external world and the stream of objective life. The human spirit alone exists, and in that alone is the writer interested. Strakhov, who knew Dostoievsky intimately, writes of him: "All his attention was upon people, and all his efforts were directed towards understanding their nature and character. People, their temperament, way of living, feelings, thoughts, these were his sole preoccupation." Again, when Dostoievsky made a journey abroad: "He did not take much count either of natural beauty or historical memories or of works of art." Certainly in all his novels he shows us towns, with their slums, low taverns, and stinking tenements; but a town is an environment in which man lives, an episode in his history, impregnated by him, the painted scenery against which he moves. When he uproots himself and turns his back on nature he falls into the detestable holes of the cities and is immersed in their beastliness—the city is the scene of the human tragedy. Petersburg, for example, which Dostoievsky apprehended and depicted in such an amazing fashion; Petersburg is a spectral vision begotten by erring and apostate men; crazy thoughts are born and criminal schemes ripen in the midst of its fogs. In such an atmosphere everything is concentrated in men, and in men who have been torn from their divine origins; their whole surround-

ings, the town and its particular atmosphere, the
lodging-houses with their monstrous appointments,
the dirty, smelly shops, the external plots of the
novels, are so many signs and symbols of the inner
spiritual world of men, a reflection of its tragedy.
Nothing exterior, whether it belonged to nature,
to society, or to manners and customs, had any
reality in itself for Dostoievsky. His drink-shops
where the "Russian boys" discuss the problems of
the universe are themselves only projections of the
human spirit and of the ideological dialectic that is
bound up with its destiny; all the complications of
the story, the external diversity of the persons who
are mutually attracted or repelled distractedly in a
gale of passion, reflect the inner deeps of that same
unique spirit: they are necessary in order to make
clear the hidden moments of destiny, but the
human riddle remains the centre.

Dostoievsky's novels are all built up around a
central figure, whether the secondary characters
converge towards it or the reverse. This chief figure
always represents a puzzle which everybody tries to
solve. *A Raw Youth*, for example, one of the most
remarkable and least appreciated of the novels, is
entirely concerned with the extraordinarily attractive figure of Versilov; it seems as if everything in the
book exists in relation to him and to the aversion or
liking which he inspires. The other characters have
no object or business except to find out the secret

of his personality and strange fate, they cannot rest until they have unravelled the mystery of Versilov's nature—it is their only real and human concern. Indeed, it would seem to the ordinary observer that all Dostoievsky's characters are "unemployed": the relationships that they have one with another are their principal business in life; but, after all, the infinitely diverse relations among men are the most important business in the human kingdom, and in Dostoievsky's books there is no need to look for any other.

The chief figure is the centre of a whirlpool of passions which is swirled up from the volcanic depths of human nature. The exclusive occupation of the "raw youth," Versilov's natural son, his concern from morning till night, is to run from one person to another trying to learn his father's secret and to clear up the mystery of his personality. A matter of the greatest seriousness, for each one is convinced of Versilov's importance and struck by his contradictory and irrational nature. The riddle is presented to us as that of his life, but actually it is the riddle of all human destiny: the contradictory, irrational, complex character of Versilov is the character of man in general. That is why there is nothing in the book apart from or without reference to him: the whole thing is an incarnation of his own inner destiny.

The same centralized construction is found in *The*

Possessed, Stravroguin being the fixed star to which all is referred and the mystery of him the subject of the book: Shatov, Verhovensky, Kirilov are no more than fragments of his disaggregated personality. The revolutionary obsession with which this book is filled represents a moment in his history and symbolizes his inner activity, his wilfulness. According to Dostoievsky, the inmost part of being cannot express itself in the stable conditions of everyday life; it comes to the light of day only in some flare-up in which the fixed and dead forms of an effete society are destroyed. Dostoievsky shows us the mazes of human contradiction which artists of another type hide behind the veil of social life, and the uncovering of these realms may well lead men to disaster, for they lie beyond the regulations made of old for the harmony of the world.

The *Idiot* differs from *A Raw Youth* and *The Possessed*. Here the action is not directed towards the central figure, Prince Muishkin, but goes out from him towards the others. It is he who explains all the riddles, especially those of two women, Aglae and Nastasia Philippovna; he helps them, he is full of prophetical foresight and intuitive clearsightedness, and he gives himself up entirely to human relationship. The storm whirls around him, but he lives in a rapture of quietness. The enigmatic and irrational principle, truly "dæmoniacal," embodied in Stavroguin and Versilov heats the atmosphere around them and produces a fiendish excitement. The principle of Muishkin's nature, equally irrational but "angelical," does not of itself cause obsession but it is powerless to exorcize it, for all that he longs with his whole soul to be a healer. Muishkin is not fully a man in the sense that Dostoievsky gives to the term; his nature is fundamentally seraphic, but deficient. Later on Dostoievsky tried to show a complete man, in Alyosha. It is worth noticing among his heroes that the "sons of darkness" (Stavroguin, Versilov, Ivan Karamazov) are the ones whom others try to fathom, towards whom action tends, while the "light-bearers" (Muishkin, Alyosha) themselves understand others and are the point of departure for action. Alyosha understands Ivan ("Ivan is a puzzle"), Muishkin reads the souls of Nastasia Philippovna and Aglae. The "light-bearers" have the gift of prophecy and try to help their fellows; the "sons of darkness" all share an enigmatical nature which is a source of trouble and disturbance to those about them. This notion of a centrifugal and centripetal movement among human beings runs through all the novels.

Crime and Punishment is different from the books mentioned above. In it human destiny is not worked out collectively in the restless surroundings of personal relations; Raskolnikov discovers the bounds of human nature by communing with and making his experiments upon himself. He is a child of darkness, but there is nothing enigmatical about him as about Stavroguin or Ivan. He represents a less advanced stage upon the road of human wilfulness, he has not yet reached their degree of complexity. It is not Raskolnikov who is a puzzle, it is his crime, in which the man exceeds his own limitations. But perverse inclination has not yet radically modified human nature in him. Raskolnikov, like the hero of *Letters from the Underworld*, puts forward problems and riddles: Versilov, Ivan Karamazov, Stavroguin are themselves these problems and riddles.

Dostoievsky was more than anything else an anthropologist, an experimentalist in human nature, who formulated a new science of man and applied to it a method of investigation hitherto unknown. His artistic science or, if it be preferred, his scientific art studied that nature in its endless convolutions and limitless extent, uncovering its lowest and most hidden layers. He subjected man to a spiritual experiment, putting him into unusual situations and then taking away all external stays one after another till his whole social framework had gone. Dostoievsky pursued his study according to the methods of dionysian art, and when he made his way into the deep places of human nature he took his whirlwinds with him. His work is an anthropology-in-motion in which things are seen in such an atmosphere of flame and ecstasy that they have meaning only for those who are themselves involved in the tempest. He leads us into the pitch darkness of man's innermost recesses—and there a glimmer of light must be found. Dostoievsky wants to kindle that spark. So he takes man and emancipates him completely, from law, from the cosmic order, and follows up his destiny in this state of freedom until he reveals whither it has inevitably led him. That was what interested Dostoievsky: what happens to man when, having liberty, he must needs turn aside to arbitrary self-will. Only then can the depth of human nature be seen; all the while existence is normal and firmly established it remains hidden, so Dostoievsky's interest begins from the moment that man sets himself up against the objective established order of the universe, cuts himself off from nature and his organic roots, and manifests his arbitrary will. When he has repudiated nature and the organized life he casts himself into the hell of the city and there treads his miserable path in expiation of his sin.

It is very instructive to compare the respective conceptions of man of Dante, Shakespeare, and Dostoievsky. For Dante (as for St. Thomas Aquinas) man is an organic part of the objective order of the world, the divine cosmos. He is one of the grades in the universal hierarchy: Heaven is above him, Hell below; God and Satan are realities belonging to the universal order, imposed on man from without, and the seven circles of Hell with their terrifying torment serve only to confirm the existence of this objective divine order. God and Satan, Heaven and Hell are not revealed within the human spirit and by human experience: they are given to man from outside and they have a reality equal to that of objects in the material world. This conception of the world, of which Dante was so great an interpreter, is strictly in line with that of the men of antiquity, and man's faith in the heaven with its hierarchical choirs above and the gehenna below was not shaken until the Renaissance. From that time on there is an absolutely new notion of the world. When the humanist era was established, with its self-affirmation and shutting-up of man within the walls of nature, Heaven and Hell were closed—but an infinity of worlds was opened. There was no longer a single cosmos with an ordered hierarchy; the infinite empty sky of the astronomers was not like Dante's sky, the mediaeval heaven, and that terror which Pascal experienced before "endless space" may be understood: man was lost in those vast solitudes which were no longer subject to any cosmic order. So he turned inward to himself, entering the psychic realm, and took refuge more and more in the earth, frightened of being separated from her in face of that new and strange infinitude.

This is the humanistic period of modern times, in the course of which man's creative forces have been played out. He is no longer bound by any objective world-order, given from above: he feels free. This is

the Renaissance, and Shakespeare was one of its
greatest geniuses. His work set forth for the first
time the psychic human world, endlessly complex
and varied, full of emotion and passion, strength and
energy, boiling over with the play of man's powers.
The heaven and hell of Dante have no place in
Shakespeare's work, which, especially with respect
to the place man holds in it, was determined by the
humanistic conception of the world, a conception
directed towards its psychic and not its spiritual
aspect, away from man's ultimate spiritual self. Man
renounced the centre of his soul and remained at the
periphery. Shakespeare, a superb psychologist, was
the psychologist of humanist art.

Dostoievsky appeared at another epoch and further stage in the history of mankind. For him, too,
man does not belong to the objective world-order of
which Dante's man was a part. During the course of
the modern period man had tried to confine himself
to the surface of the earth and to enclose himself
within a purely human universe. God and Satan,
Heaven and Hell were definitively relegated to the
regions of the unknowable as having no communi-
cation with this world, until at length they were
deprived of all reality. Man himself became a flat
creature in two dimensions—he had lost that of
depth; his soul was left to him but his spirit had
gone. But the time came when the creative and
joyous energy that marked the Renaissance dried up,

and man began to feel that the earth was not so solid
under his feet as he had thought: sudden rumb-
lings were heard and the volcanic nature of the
underworld was manifested.   In man himself an
abyss opened and therein God and Heaven, the
Devil and Hell were revealed anew.   At first one
could only grope about in these depths, for the daylight of the world of the soul and of her material
earth was fading and the abrupt kindling of a new
light had not yet taken place.

The modern age served its apprenticeship to
human freedom and man's powers were given full
opportunity, but at the end of that period this experiment in liberty was carried over to another plane
and another dimension, and it is there that man's
destiny is now working itself out.   Human freedom
abandoned the psychic world in whose daylight it
had existed since the Renaissance and plunged into
the depths of the spiritual world.   It is like a descent
into Hell.   But there man will find again not only
Satan and his kingdom, but also God and Heaven;
and they will no longer be revealed in accordance
with an objective order imposed from without but
by way of a face-to-face meeting with the ultimate
depths of the human spirit, as an inwardly revealed
reality.   All Dostoievsky's work is an illustration of
this.   Therein man has a very different place from
that given to him by Dante or Shakespeare: he
neither forms part of an unchangeable objective

D—d

order nor exists on the surface of the earth or of his own soul. Spiritual life is restored to him, and he has found it in himself: that is to say that, according to Dostoievsky, the spiritual life is imminent in man and not transcendent. But it must be clearly understood that this does not imply that he denied all transcendental reality.

The first manifestations of newly-freed man are exaggerated individualism, self-isolation, and rebellion against the exterior harmony of the world; he develops an unhealthy self-love which moves him to explore the lower regions of his being. He begins to burrow from the surface of the earth, and "underworld man,"* a shapeless, ugly creature, makes his appearance and exhibits his dialectic.

In the *Letters from the Underworld* Dostoievsky made many things clear about human nature. It is extreme, antinomian, and irrational; man is overwhelmingly attracted towards unreasonableness, towards a lawless freedom, towards suffering. He is not necessarily acquisitive, and at any moment may capriciously choose suffering rather than profit. He does not adapt himself to a rational organization of life and he puts freedom before happiness. But this freedom is not the primacy of reason over the psychic

* The original has *podpolya* (from *pol,* floor, and *pod,* under), meaning the space between the floor and the ground or between a floor and the ceiling beneath. The word is associated with the idea of vermin breeding in the darkness and preparing destruction. TR.

element; rather is it irrational and senseless to the highest degree, enticing him beyond his proper limits. This unlimited liberty is a torment and ruination to man, but its pain and disaster are dear to him. These discoveries of Dostoievsky in the "dungeons" of human being determine the destiny of Raskolnikov, of Stavroguin, of Ivan Karamazov, and the rest. Man's painful pilgrimage along the ways of arbitrary liberty lead him to the uttermost limits of inner division.

This dialectic of the destiny of mankind which Dostoievsky began in *Letters from the Underworld* is developed throughout his novels and reaches its height in the Legend of the Grand Inquisitor. Ivan Karamazov is the last stage on the road of wilfulness and rebellion against God; after him only appear Zosima and Alyosha. We shall see how this tragic dialectic is resolved in the Legend by the image of Christ. How did it begin?

"Underworld man" refuses any organization based on harmony and universal happiness. "I shall not be a bit surprised," says the hero of the *Letters from the Underworld*, "if in the midst of this Universal Reason that is to be there will appear, all of a sudden and unexpectedly, some common-faced, or rather cynical and sneering, gentleman who with his arms akimbo will say to us: 'Now then, you fellows, what about smashing all this Reason to bits, sending their logarithms to the devil, and living as we like accord-

ing *to our own silly will?* † That might not be much, but
the annoying thing is that he would immediately get
plenty of followers—men are made like that. And
the cause of all this is so absurd that it would scarcely
seem worth speaking of: man, whoever he is and
wherever he is to be found, prefers to act as he wills
than as reason and interest dictate. One may will
against one's own interest—sometimes one has to.
Scope for free choice, personal caprice, however
extravagant, the maddest of fancies—those are what
man is after, quintessential objects that you can't
classify and in exchange for which all systems and
theories can go to hell. Where then have all these
wiseacres found that man's will should primarily be
normal and virtuous? Why have they imagined that
man needs a will directed towards reason and his
own benefit? All he needs is an *independent* will, what-
ever it may cost him and wherever it may lead him.
. . . In only one single case does man consciously
and deliberately want something absurd, and that is
the silliest thing of all, namely, to *have the right* to
want the absurd and not to be bound by the necessity of wanting only what is reasonable. Moreover,
gentlemen, in certain circumstances an absurdity, a
foolish caprice, can be more advantageous to our
neighbour than anything else in the world. It is
useful even if it involves evident harm, if it contra-

† Here and elsewhere the dagger† indicates that the italics are
M. Berdyaev's.

dicts the sanest conclusions of our judgment about what constitutes our own interests, for at all events *it will have safeguarded our dearest and most essential possession—our personality and individuality.*"† Man is not an arithmetical expression; he is a mysterious and puzzling being, and his nature is extreme and contradictory all through. "What can one expect from a being endowed with such strange qualities as man? He goes after the most harmful follies and the most unpractical absurdity simply and solely to mix up positive reason with the pernicious element of his fancy; in fact, he emphasizes his capriciousness and stupidity in order to persuade himself that people are people and not the keys of a piano. . . ."

"If you say that everything, chaos, darkness, anathema, can be reduced to mathematical formulae, that it is possible to anticipate all things and keep them under the sway of reason by means of an arithmetical calculation, then man will go insane on purpose so as to have no judgement and to behave as he likes. I believe this because it appears *that man's whole business is to prove to himself that he is a man and not a cog-wheel.*† . . . What will become of free will when everything is in terms of the multiplication-table and the only thing left is the notion that 2 and 2 make 4? 2 and 2 will make 4 without the help of my will. Does the will consist in that? . . ."

"Does not man revel in destruction and confusion because he instinctively dreads that he may attain

his end and crown the work he has begun? And perhaps—who knows?—the end of mankind on earth
may consist in this uninterrupted striving after
something ahead, that is, in life itself, rather than in
some real end which obviously must be a static
formula of the same kind as '2 and 2 make 4.' *For
2 and 2 make 4 is not a part of life but the beginning of
death.†* . . . And why are you so firmly and solemnly
convinced that only that which is normal and positive, in a word, his well-being, is good for man? Is
the reason never deceived about what is beneficial?
It is possible that, as well as loving his own welfare,
man is fond of suffering, even passionately fond of
it. . . . I am sure that man will never renounce the
genuine suffering that comes of ruin and chaos. Why,
suffering is the one and only source of knowledge."

These reflections of genius, startling in the light
they throw, are the origin of all the things that
Dostoievsky in his work as a creator found out about
man. The methods to apply to man are not those
of arithmetic but of the higher mathematics, for his
destiny does not depend on such an elementary
truth as that 2 and 2 make 4. Human nature cannot
be brought within the operations of reason: there is
always "something over," an irrational something
which is the very well-spring of life. And human
society can never be "rationalized," because there is
an irrational principle in it; it is not a nest of ants,
but to deny that freedom which urges every man to

"live in his own silly way" is to treat it as such. The "gentleman with a cynical and sneering face" represents the revolt of the personality and the individualistic principle, the uprising of a liberty that will tolerate the yoke neither of reason nor of an obligatory welfare. Here we can already see Dostoievsky's profound antagonism to Socialism, to the Crystal Palace, to an earthly paradise, which he was to develop to the utmost in *The Possessed* and *The Brothers Karamazov*: man must not let himself be turned into a part of a machine. Dostoievsky always had a very exalted idea of personality, which, indeed, was fundamental to his conception of the world, and with the notion of "person" he joined the problem of immortality, which for him was essential. His masterly criticism of social eudemonism is directed towards demonstrating its incompatibility with the independence and dignity of personality.

Was Dostoievsky himself among the underworld men? Did he make their dialectic his own? This question can only be considered dynamically. The underground man's conception of the world is not the positive religious conception that Dostoievsky had, the conception in which he made plain the dangerousness of the arbitrary ways and rebellion in which underworld men were engaged because they were heading for the destruction of human freedom and the decomposition of personality. But underworld man and his astounding dialectic of irrational liberty represent a moment on the tragic road whereon mankind tries out and experiences freedom; for freedom is the supreme good: man cannot renounce it without renouncing himself and ceasing to be a man. So Dostoievsky in his conception of the world rejected what underworld man rejected in his dialectic. To the very end he refused to rationalize human society and repudiated all attempts to exalt happiness, reason, and well-being above liberty; he would have nothing to do with the Great Exhibition or any anticipated harmony based on the ruins of human personality. Instead he wanted to take men along the ways of wildest self-will and revolt in order to show them that they lead to the extinction of liberty and to self-annihilation. This road of liberty can only end either in the deification of man or in the discovery of God; in the one case, he is lost and done for; in the other, he finds salvation and the definitive confirmation of himself as God's earthly image. For man does not exist unless there be a God and unless he be the image and likeness of God; if there be no God, then man deifies himself, ceases to be man, and his own image perishes. The only solution to the problem of man is in Jesus Christ. So the underworld dialectic is only the point of departure of Dostoievsky's own, which did not reach its conclusion till *The Brothers Karamazov*. But one point already is clear: in Dostoievsky's view, man cannot return to that idea of an obligatory and imposed reason against which underworld man has risen; he must pass through the test of freedom. And Dostoievsky shows, as we have seen, that if man is forced into rational moulds and his life fenced about with formulae he "will go insane on purpose so as to have no judgment and behave as he likes." According to him, a certain "fantasticalness" or eccentricity is an essential element in human nature, and Stavroguin, Versilov, Ivan Karamazov are "enigmatical" because that nature is itself puzzling—in its antinomies, its irrationality, its taste for suffering.

Dostoievsky's anthropology shows human nature to be in the highest degree dynamic. Immobility is only a surface characteristic; the veil of custom and the harmony of the soul hide whirling storms, with which alone he was concerned, and he went down into these gloomy depths and unsealed a fountain of light, light more authentic than that which shines on the untroubled surface. Man's stormy restlessness is due to the polarity of his nature, to the shock of colliding contraries. Dostoievsky, unlike Plato and a large number of mystics, did not believe that the calm of eternity is to be found in the depths of the soul: unity and quiet are not there but passionate agitation, for polarity, antinomy, is the radical characteristic of human nature. And this ceaseless motion is not confined to the surface of being; the collisions of contradiction have place in

the life of the spirit as well as of the body and soul.
That is an essential point in Dostoievsky's anthropology and ontology. He is opposed to the aesthetic
conception of Hellenism and belongs to the world of
Christianity wherein the tragic dynamism of being
is revealed. Moreover, the Slav or Russian genius
differs in its notion of the ultimates of being from the
Germanic as it is expressed in idealist philosophy.
The German tends to see the conflict between God
and Satan, light and darkness, only on the superficial plane, at the periphery of the spirit; when he
goes below that he finds God, light: all antinomy
disappears. But for the Russian Dostoievsky it is
the other way round; evil also has a spiritual nature,
and the battle between the divine and hellish elements is carried on deep down in the spirit of man:
he finds the antagonism of the two principles in the
very essence of being and not in the psychic domain
where it may be seen by all. Accordingly, the
terms "divine" and "diabolic" did not connote the
exterior ideas of "good" and "evil" for Dostoievsky.
If he had developed his teaching about God and the
Absolute to its necessary conclusion he would have
had to acknowledge an antinomy in the nature even
of God, to have found in him also a chasm of darkness, thus approximating to Jacob Boehme's theory
of the *Ungrund*. The human heart is in essence antinomian, but it dwells in a fathomless abyss of being.

To Dostoievsky is due the striking phrase that

"beauty will save the world." He knew nothing higher than beauty, it is the supreme expression of ontological perfection, divine—but it is also antinomian, divided, impassioned, terrifying; it has not the godlike calm of the platonic ideal but is scorching, variable, full of tragic conflict. Beauty did not appear to him in the cosmic order, on the divine plane, but through man, and so it shares the eternal unrest of mankind and is borne along the stream of Heraclitus. We are reminded of Mitya Karamazov's words: "Beauty is a terrible and frightening thing. It is terrible because it has not been fathomed, and can't be fathomed, for God makes nothing but riddles. And in this one extremes meet and contraries lie down together. . . . Beauty! I can't bear to think that a man of fine mind and noble heart begins with the ideal of our Lady and ends with the ideal of Sodom. More horrifying still is that a man with the ideal of Sodom in his soul does not renounce the ideal of our Lady; it goes on glowing in his heart, quite genuinely, just as it did when he was young and innocent. Man is too broad; I'd make him narrower." And again: "Beauty is mysterious as well as terrible. God and the Devil are fighting there, and the battlefield is the human heart." In the same way Nicholas Stavroguin "found the same beauty and an equal delight at the two opposed poles"; there was a similar attraction for him in the ideal of our Lady and the ideal of Sodom. Dostoievsky was profoundly troubled that beauty should be found in both these things at once, and his mind misgave him that there is a satanic element in beauty. His conviction of the antinomy in human nature was so strong that, as we shall see, he found this dark and evil element even in human love.

Dostoievsky appeared at the moment when modern times were coming to an end and a new epoch of history was dawning, and it is likely that his consciousness of the inner division of human nature and its movement towards the ultimate depths of being was closely related to this fact. It was given to him to reveal the struggle in man between the God-man and the man-god,* between Christ and Antichrist, a conflict unknown to preceding ages when wickedness was seen in only its most elementary and simple forms. To-day the soul of man no longer rests upon secure foundations, everything round him is unsteady and contradictory, he lives in an atmosphere of illusion and falsehood under a ceaseless threat of *change*. Evil comes forward under an appearance of good, and he is deceived; the faces of Christ and of Antichrist, of man become god and of God become man, are interchangeable. A good example is provided by the work of Merejkovsky, who could not

* Russians speak of the man-god, or superman, meaning thereby the incarnation of the spirit of Antichrist and of opposition to our Lord involved in man's self-deification.

with certainty tell Christ from Antichrist; his book on Tolstoy and Dostoievsky, notable for several reasons, is full of this dualism and perpetual confusion.

A large number of contemporary people have "divided minds." They are the sort of folk whom Dostoievsky displayed to us, and it is not the slightest use trying to apply the old moral catechism to them— access to their souls is a far more complicated business. It is the destiny of such people over whom the waves of an apocalyptic environment are breaking that Dostoievsky set himself to study, and the light he shed upon them was truly marvellous. Far-reaching discoveries about human nature in general can be made when mankind is undergoing a spiritual and religious crisis, and it was precisely such a time when Dostoievsky appeared upon the scene; he marks an absolutely new stage in anthropological knowledge, one that is neither humanist nor yet Christian in the traditional sense of the fathers of the Church.

He was not content to rediscover *the old and eternal Christian truth about man,* which had decayed and been forgotten during the humanist era. The experiment of Humanism and the experience of freedom had not been in vain, a negative quantity in man's history. A new soul had been born, one with new doubts and a new knowledge of evil but also with new horizons, new perspectives, and a thirst for new relations with

God: man had reached a more advanced state of spiritual maturity. So we find that the profoundly Christian anthropology of Dostoievsky differs from patristic anthropology. The science of man known to the fathers and doctors of the Church, the understanding of the ways of mankind that can be discerned in the writings and lives of the saints, was no longer sufficient to answer all man's questions or to understand all the doubts and temptations that beset his new stage of spiritual growth. Man has not become better, he is not nearer to God, but his soul has become much more complicated and his spirit has grown bitter. Certainly the Christian soul of the past knew sin and let itself fall under the dominion of Satan, but it did not know that rift in the personality that troubles the people that Dostoievsky studied. In times past evil was more obvious and more simple, and it would be difficult to heal a contemporary soul of its disease by yesterday's remedies alone. Dostoievsky understood that. He knew all that Nietzsche was to know, but with something added; whereas his contemporary, the hermit Theophanes, a high authority among Russian Orthodox ascetics and spiritual writers, did not know what Dostoievsky and Nietzsche knew and therefore could not deal with the misery engendered by mankind's fresh experiences. The thing which Dostoievsky and Nietzsche knew is that man is terribly free, that liberty is tragic and a grievous burden to him. They had seen the parting of the ways in front of mankind, one road leading to the God-man, Jesus Christ, the other to self-deification, the man-god; they had seen the human soul at the moment when God was withdrawn from it and so undergoing a religious experience of a very special kind, which after a long period of wandering in darkness will produce a new enlightenment. That is how the Christianity of Dostoievsky differs radically from that of Theophanes, and why the *startzi* of the monastery of Optina did not acknowledge him as fully theirs after reading *The Brothers Karamazov*. Dostoievsky found that the road to Christ led through illimitable freedom, but he showed that on it also lurked the lying seductions of Antichrist and the temptation to make a god of man. True or not, Dostoievsky had said something new about man.

Dostoievsky's work marked not merely a crisis in but the defeat of Humanism, and in this his name should be bracketed with Nietzsche's. They have made it impossible to go back to the old rationalistic Humanism with its self-affirmation and sufficiency, for it is shown that the way, whether to Christ or Antichrist, lies further on and that man cannot remain simply man. Kirilov wanted to be God; Nietzsche wanted to overcome man as a shame and a disgrace, and turned towards the superman; thus the last end of the humanist cult of man is found to be his own destruction by absorption in the superman. So far from being safeguarded, he is pushed aside as something disgusting, puny, null, fit only to be a means to the superman, that magic idol that devours the men who kneel before him and every other human thing as well.

It may be said then that European Humanism found its term in Nietzsche, who was flesh of its flesh, blood of its blood, and victim of its sins. There was a great difference between him and Dostoievsky who, before him, had shown that the loss of man by the way of self-deification was the inevitable goal of Humanism. Dostoievsky recognized that this deification is illusory, he explored the vagaries of self-will in every direction, and he had another source of knowledge—he saw the light of Christ: he was a prophet of the Spirit. Nietzsche, on the contrary, was dominated by his idea of the superman and it killed the idea of real man in him. Only Christianity has cherished and protected the idea of mankind and fixed the human image for ever and ever. The human essence presupposes the divine essence; kill God, and at the same time you kill man, and on the grave of these two supreme ideas of God and of man there is set up a monstrous image—the image of the man who wants to be God, of the superman in action, of Antichrist. For Nietzsche there was neither God nor man but only this unknown man-god. For Dostoievsky there was both God and man: the God who does not devour man and the man who is not dissolved in God but remains himself throughout all eternity. It is there that Dostoievsky shows himself to be a Christian in the deepest sense of the word.

It is surprising that the dionysiac ecstasy did not involve him in a destructive negation of the human form and individuality, for the pagan Dionysism of Greece went to the excess of swallowing up the individual in the great impersonal stream of nature; dionysian delirium is in general disastrous to personality. But no excitement or ecstasy could shake Dostoievsky into a denial of man, and that was the trait that made his anthropology a quite new and special phenomenon. Up till then the human appearance, the features of personality, were linked to a formal element, while Dionysism, on the other hand, supposed the abolition of the principle of personality altogether. It was otherwise with Dostoievsky. He was exclusively dionysiac, but the human person was affirmed with all the more strength in the heart of his exaltation; man, with all his dynamism and contradictions, remained himself all through, indestructibly man. Here Dostoievsky avoided not only Greek Dionysism but also the mysticism of the many Christians for whom man vanished and left only the divine. Man has a part in eternity, and when Dostoievsky explored the deep places of life he came upon those of God as well. All his work is a plea for man. He was in radical opposition to the

E—d

monophysite* spirit: he recognized not one single nature, human or divine, but two natures, human and divine. He took such a strong line on this point that, compared with his, the Eastern Orthodox and Catholic conception seems almost to smack of monophysism, to suggest an inclination to absorb the human in the divine nature.

Dostoievsky was bound to man more than any thinker before him had been; he safeguarded the image and likeness of God in the least and most abandoned of his creatures. But his love for man was not the love of the humanists: it was composed of infinite sympathy with a certain admixture of "cruelty," and he foretold the path of man's suffering, in accordance with that part of his anthropology that had reference to the idea of freedom. Without freedom there is no man, and Dostoievsky conducted all his dialectic on man and his destiny as the dialectic of the destiny of freedom. Now the way of freedom is the way of suffering, and man must follow it to the end. Therefore fully to understand Dostoievsky's teaching on man it is necessary to examine what he had to say about freedom and evil.

* The historical heresy of Monophysism, condemned alike by the Catholic and the Orthodox Churches, has reference to the two natures in Christ, not to the existence of two natures as such. Tr.

CHAPTER III

FREEDOM

IT is surprising that it has not hitherto been sufficiently noticed that for Dostoievsky the theme of man and his destiny is in the first place the theme of freedom, that freedom is the centre of his conception of the world, that his hidden pathos is a pathos of freedom. Many passages can be quoted from the *Diary of a Writer* in which he seems to be opposed to political liberty in general and refers to himself as conservative, even reactionary, and these external characteristics have hindered people from seeing that freedom is the kernel of his work and the key to the understanding of his philosophy. What has been called his "cruelty" is directly associated with this. He was "cruel" because he would not relieve man of his burden of freedom, he would not deliver him from suffering at the price of such a loss, he insisted that man must accept an enormous responsibility corresponding to his dignity as a free being. It is possible that man's sufferings could be lightened by depriving him of liberty, and in the course of his thorough exploration of this possibility Dostoievsky made some very important observations. For him the justification both of God and of man must be looked for in freedom, of which the tragic process of the world is only a function, its issue subordinate to the progress of the main theme. So he studied the destiny of man exclusively in freedom and the destiny of freedom in man. All his novels—his tragedies —are concerned with the experiment of human liberty. Man begins to rebel in its name, ready for any misery or madness provided he can feel free. And at the same time he pursues his quest for the uttermost and final freedom.

There are two sorts of freedom, initial and final, and between the two stretches man's road, beset with suffering, the road of inner division. St. Augustine, also, in his campaign against Pelagianism had taught that there were two freedoms, *libertas minor* and *libertas maior*. The lesser freedom was the beginning, freedom to choose the good, which supposes the possibility of sin; the greater freedom was the ending, freedom in God, in the bosom of good. Augustine was the apologist of the second and greater freedom, and he at last reached the doctrine of predestination which, though the Church has modified it where it concerns freedom, may nevertheless be said to have had an influence on Catholicism unfavourable to freedom. Anyway, it is certain that there are two freedoms and not one only, the first to choose between good and evil, the last in the heart of good—an irrational freedom and a freedom within reason. Socrates knew only the second of these, and the words of the gospel, "You shall know the truth, and the truth shall make you free," also refer to it, the freedom in Christ. That is the freedom that we have in view when it is said that man ought to free himself from lower influences, to have control of his passions, to throw off enslavement to himself and to his environment, and the highest desire for freedom of spirit aims at it.

The freedom of the first Adam and the freedom in Christ of the second Adam are different. The truth shall make men free, but they must freely accept it and not be brought to it by force. Our Lord gives man the final liberty, but man must first freely have cleaved to him: "Thou didst desire man's free love, that he should follow thee freely, a willing captive"— they are the words of the Grand Inquisitor. It is this free choice of Christ that constitutes the Christian's dignity and gives meaning to his act of faith, which is above all a free act. The dignity of man and the dignity of faith require the recognition of two freedoms, freedom to choose the truth and freedom in the truth. Freedom cannot be identified with goodness or truth or perfection: it is by nature autonomous, it is freedom and not goodness. Any identification or confusion of freedom with goodness and perfection involves a negation of freedom and a strengthening of methods of compulsion; obligatory goodness ceases to be goodness by the fact of its constraint. But free goodness, which alone is true, entails the liberty of evil. That is the tragedy that Dostoievsky saw and studied, and it contains the mystery of Christianity.

Its dialectic works out thus: Free goodness involves the freedom of evil; but freedom of evil leads to the destruction of freedom itself and its degeneration into an evil necessity. On the other hand, the denial of the freedom of evil in favour of an exclusive freedom of good ends equally in a negation of freedom and its degeneration—into a good necessity. But a good necessity is not good, because goodness resides in freedom from necessity.

This problem has haunted Christian thought throughout its history. It can be found bound up with St. Augustine's struggle against Pelagianism, with the disputes about the relations between liberty and grace and with those provoked by Jansenism, with Luther's denial of man's freedom, with Calvin's sombre predestinarianism. The spectres of a bad liberty and a good compulsion have dogged the steps of Christian thinkers and freedom has suffered, sometimes through the evil found in it, sometimes by way of enforced goodness. The fires of the Inquisition were the horrifying evidence of this tragedy of freedom and the difficulty found in its resolution even by a conscience enlightened by the light of Christ. Denial of the first liberty, to believe or not to believe, to accept truth or to reject it, leads inevitably to the doctrine of the predestinarians. That truth attracts to itself without the intervention of freedom is a dangerous illusion. And Eastern Orthodoxy, though very well-disposed towards liberty, has not recognized sufficiently that freedom contains a truth that has yet to be discovered. There is truth about freedom as well as freedom in truth, and the answer to its everlasting problem should be sought in the fact that Christ is not only the Truth, but *the truth about freedom*, unconstrained truth, that he is himself freedom and unconstrained love. In dealing with freedom there is a strong tendency to mix up its formal and material elements. Those who already have the second and greater freedom have in effect tried to set aside the first, free choice of good or evil, as a purely formal freedom; their intransigent truthfulness cannot bear the possibility of error. But this liberty of conscience in the choice of good or bad is a material liberty, and Dostoievsky showed that it is a part of Christianity, for Christianity accepts the whole of freedom—otherwise it would have to renounce the possession of that truth of freedom which is the very truth of Jesus Christ.

Christianity is the religion of freedom and in its essence and content recognizes it in all its forms; and in Christianity as Dostoievsky understood it the tragic principle of freedom is victor over the principle of compulsion. Divine grace itself is a complete freedom that can be destroyed neither by evil nor by the constraint of the good; God's freedom and man's freedom are reconciled in the grace of freely-given love. The divine truth of Christ has shone upon that first freedom, of choice between good and evil, and shown it to be an inalienable part of itself; the freedom of the human spirit and conscience is a part of Christian truth. In the opinion of Dostoievsky, Christian teachers have not hitherto made this clear enough and he made a valiant attempt to supply the deficiency.

Dostoievsky attributed to man the ability to tread the road of truth which would lead him through the darkness and horrors of division and catastrophe to a definitive freedom. The way is neither direct nor clear and man will go astray on it, deceived by phantasms and will-o'-the-wisps. Doubtless this long passage through the experience of good and evil could be made much shorter and easier by limiting or even entirely suppressing human liberty. But what is the value of men coming to God otherwise than by the road of freedom and after having experienced the harmfulness of evil? Are they not less welcome to him? Is not the whole meaning of the universal historical process to be found in this divine thirst to receive the *free* love of man? But man is slow in his movement of love towards God. He has first to undergo bitter disillusionments and taste the disappointments of love for unworthy objects. The grace which God gives us is not irresistibly imposed, but is a helping and sustaining grace, and every time that Christian men have tried to make of its strength an instrument of force and coercion they have erred towards the paths of Antichrist. Dostoievsky set out this Christian truth of the freedom of the human spirit with unprecedented penetration.

Freedom was a gift of Christianity to a redeemed mankind. It was not known to Greece and the ancient East, where man was bound by necessity, by the order of nature, by fate. Christianity gave him full freedom, both initial and final, the freedom of the first Adam as well as of the second, of choice of evil as well as of good. Greek thought admitted only of a rational freedom; but Christianity found in it a non-rational principle which is manifest in the very stuff of life and contains the whole mystery of liberty. Hellenic consciousness dreaded this irrational element, bearer of the infinite, of the ἄπειρον πηρός, and opposed it from the point of view of form and finality: the Greek conceived the world as bounded by form within limits, without suspecting the infinite spaces beyond. In the Christian world man no longer feared the unbounded and inexhaustible content of life, for the limitless vistas of the infinite had been opened to him, and that is why the Christian attitude to freedom is quite different from that of the man of antiquity. Freedom sets itself up against the exclusive domination of the formal element and the building of barriers; it presupposes the infinite. That meant chaos to a Greek; so it does to a Christian, but it means freedom as well, and infinite human aspirations are possible only in a Christian world. Faust is inconceivable in the ancient world: his endless velleities are characteristic of Christian Europe, and nowhere else could Byron have given us *Manfred, Cain,* and *Don Juan.* Liberty in revolt, tumultuous aspirations without end, the irrational element in life, these are phenomena of the Christian world, and the uprising of human personality against world-organization and control is an interiorly Christian manifestation. Greek tragedy and the best of Greek philosophy had shown the need to pull down the barriers that shut their world in and thus pointed the way towards the new Christian dispensation; but neither the drama nor the philosophy of the Greeks knew anything about the soul of Faust and its awful freedom.

Among the characters of Dostoievsky's fiction freedom in revolt reached the highest degree of tension; they represent a new and more advanced stage than Faust in the development of human destiny as it has been carried on within Christianity. Faust was still only half way along the road; Raskolnikov, Stavroguin, Kirilov, Ivan Karamazov have reached its end. Even after Faust we can still imagine the nineteenth century going on, full of enthusiasm for

the draining of marshes; but after Dostoievsky's
heroes there is the unforeseeable twentieth century
with its promise of a cultural crisis and the end of an
era in the world's history.

The quest for human freedom entered on a new
phase. Liberty with Dostoievsky was the manifestation of a new spirit as well as of Christianity; it
belonged to a new stage of Christianity itself, which
was passing from a period essentially transcendental
to one of a greater interior penetration. Man was
escaping from external forms and by hard ways finding light within himself; everything was being carried
over into the deep places of the human spirit, and it
was there that the new world was revealed. The
transcendental conception of Christianity, by showing its truth from without as an objective truth,
failed to reveal the full extent of Christian freedom.

The figure of Christ ought to present itself to a free
man as that of an ultimate and final freedom that he
finds within himself, one that he has already used
and abused in his lesser liberty and allowed to
degenerate into its contrary. That is the tragic story
that Dostoievsky tells in his heroes: freedom deteri-
orating into self-will and a defiant self-affirmation
to be thenceforward ineffectual, worthless, and a
drain on the individual. The freedom of Stavroguin
and of Versilov is empty and meaningless; that of
Svidrigailov and of Fyodor Pavlovitch Karamazov
disintegrates the personality; that of Raskolnikov

and of Peter Verhovensky leads to crime; the daemoniac freedom of Kirilov and of Ivan Karamazov kills man. Thus freedom that is arbitrary destroys itself; there is an immanent necessity that it should lead to enslavement and change the very face of man. It is not an external punishment, a law from without that brings down its heavy hand upon the transgressor, but a divine principle within that strikes the conscience so that man is consumed as by fire amid the shadows of the wilderness that he has himself chosen.

Thus does Dostoievsky set out the fate of man and his freedom. He must tread that road, but he lets freedom become debased into servitude and at last kill him, because he is too intoxicated by it to see anything above himself—and if there is nothing above himself, then man does not exist. And if there is no content and object in freedom, if there is no bond between human freedom and divine freedom, then freedom does not exist either. If all things are allowable to man, then freedom becomes its own slave, and the man who is his own slave is lost. The human image needs the support of a higher nature, and human freedom reaches its definitive expression in a higher freedom, freedom in truth. The dialectic is irrefutable. And it draws us into the wake of God-made-man, by whom alone human freedom can be joined with divine freedom and the form of man with the form of God. The light of this truth is born of an interior experience, interiorly lived; no return is possible to the exclusive tyranny of an external law and a life of necessity and compulsion. All that is left is our once destroyed liberty re-established in truth, that is, in the heart of Christ. He is not an external law, a stream of exterior life; between his kingdom and the kingdom of this world there is no common measure: and Dostoievsky hotly denounces every tendency of Christianity to become a religion of obligation and constraint. The light of truth and the treasures of definitive freedom cannot be received from outside. And the ultimate freedom, not the aimless, rebellious, voluntarily circumscribed liberty that kills man and destroys his image but the liberty rich in fulfilment that confirms man as man unto eternity, that freedom is Christ. The fates of Raskolnikov and Stavroguin and Kirilov and Ivan Karamazov testify to the truth of this: freedom wrongly directed was the downfall of them all. That does not mean, however, that they ought to have been put under compulsion or submitted to external law and regulation. Their loss is an enlightening lesson for us, and their tragedy a hymn to freedom.

It was a controlling idea of Dostoievsky that there could be no world harmony except through an experience of freedom that embraced both good and evil, that it could not be based on compulsion, whether theocratic or socialistic. Hence his antipathy to both Socialism and Catholicism, to which he opposed liberty of the human spirit (which is in revolt, for example, in the person of "the gentleman with a cynical and sneering face"). He could acknowledge neither a paradise wherein this liberty was not yet possible nor one wherein—as it seemed to him—it had ceased to exist. The faith which he wished to see established was a free faith, buttressed by liberty of conscience; his own had "burst forth from a huge furnace of doubt" and he wanted all faith to be tried in the same fire.

The Christian world has not known a more passionate defender of liberty of conscience: "The freedom of their faith was dearer to thee than anything," says the Grand Inquisitor to Christ, and the words were as applicable to Dostoievsky himself: "Thou didst desire man's free love. . . . Man must freely decide for himself what is good and what is evil, having only thine image before him as a guide instead of the rigid law of old"—it is Dostoievsky's own profession of faith. He stigmatized "miracle, mystery, and authority" as means of bearing down man's conscience and curtailing the freedom of his spirit against which Satan directed his attacks when he tempted our Lord in the wilderness. In Christ there is no forcing of conscience: the religion of Golgotha is free; when the Son of God came into the world "in the form of a servant" and was tortured by the world on the cross he appealed to the free human spirit. He used no coercion to make us believe in him as in God, he had not the might and majesty of the sovereigns of this world, the kingdom that he preached was not here. Therein lies the radical secret of Jesus Christ, the secret of freedom. It needed an extraordinary freedom of spirit, a prodigy of free faith, a spontaneous recognition of "things not seen" to see God beneath the appearance of a bondsman, and when Simon Peter said to Jesus, "Thou art the Christ, the Son of the living God," he made an act of freedom. These words have echoed through man's consciousness, shaping the course of history, and every soul in Christendom ought to repeat them in sincerity and truth. They hold the whole dignity of Christianity.

Dostoievsky thought that this Christian freedom had been better safeguarded by Eastern Orthodoxy than by the Catholicism of the West. But he was often unjust to Catholicism and shut his eyes to the failures and defects of Orthodoxy: there was no liberty in the Byzantine imperial theocracy. But his own religion went far beyond either historical Orthodoxy or historical Catholicism in freedom of spirit. Nevertheless, he always remained a child of Russian Orthodoxy to the marrow of his bones. Christ was freedom, Antichrist was obligation, compulsion, subjection of the spirit; and in analysing the anti-Christian principle he denounced every aspect under which it may be found in history, from Eastern and Western theocracy, from imperial Caesaro-papism, to anarchism and atheistic socialism.

Raskolnikov, Stavroguin, Kirilov, Versilov, Ivan Karamazov had to pass through the furnace of doubt; the words of St. Peter—"Thou art the Christ, the Son of the living God"—must burst from the spirit and from an unconstrained conscience, and Dostoievsky knew that therein alone lay their salvation. If they could not find the strength and freedom needful to recognize Jesus as the Son of God they were doomed to perish; but if they recognized that, then the liberty of the man from the underworld would be transformed into "the liberty of the glory of the children of God." Dostoievsky began his enquiry into freedom with that of the underworld man, which seemed limitless; he examined the bounds of human nature which such men wanted to overpass. If man is free to that extent, are not all things lawful for him? Is he not entitled to commit any crime, even parricide, in virtue of some "higher principle"? Are not the ideals of our Lady and of Sodom then on the same level? May not man aspire to become himself God? In a word, is not man bound to give rein to his self-will? Dostoievsky saw that the seeds of death are in such freedom. Raskolnikov ended by confessing his own ruin and worthlessness, Stavroguin's liberty degenerated into sterility and extinction of personality; but the example of Kirilov is the most important here.

Kirilov proclaimed self-will as a duty, a sacred obligation which must be fulfilled in order that man may reach a higher state. He himself was a good man, master of his impulses and passions, a sort of saint without grace. But the best of men is on the way to disaster if he rejects God in favour of himself; he has parted with his own freedom and becomes possessed by the power of spirits whose nature he does not know. So with Kirilov. His freedom of spirit shows unmistakable symptoms of degeneration, and he is the last person to have any control over them; he has entered on the way of self-deification and it is fatal to freedom and to man himself. All Dostoievsky's heroes who are inwardly divided and given to self-will suffer the same loss. With Svidrigailov and Fyodor Pavlovitch Karamazov the ruin of personality is such that the word freedom cannot even be uttered in their respect. Dostoievsky treats of the consequences to personality of obsession by a vicious passion or iniquitous idea in a masterly fashion. A man obsessed is no longer free. Is Versilov free? His passion for Katerina Nicolaevna is an obsession: he can't separate her from himself, she destroys him, he loses the ability to choose between one idea and another—he is torn between their contradictions, he is "divided." No man who is divided can be free, and a man who cannot make the free act of choosing the object of his love is condemned to this division.

F—d

It is in the *The Brothers Karamazov* that Dostoievsky finally and definitively shows that freedom in so far as it is self-will and self-affirmation must end in a negation of God, of man and of the world, and of freedom itself. The conclusion of his dialectic is that freedom as it develops cancels itself out, compulsion and an evil necessity are lying in wait for it. The doctrines of the Grand Inquisitor and of Shigalev are born of self-will and godlessness: freedom becomes self-will, self-will becomes compulsion. That is the process. It is the self-willed who deny the freedom of a religious conscience and of the human spirit.

Once man has set his foot upon the road of self-will and self-affirmation he must sacrifice the primacy of spirit and his original freedom and become the plaything of necessity and compulsion. "Boundless liberty leads me on to boundless tyranny," says Shigalev, and that has been the evolution of all revolutionary freedom, as may be seen in the French Revolution. Capricious and arbitrary freedom, atheistic freedom, contains a germ of colossal violence and can only beget "endless tyranny" in which all guarantees of freedom are thrown to the winds. The insurgence of wilfulness and caprice makes men miss the essential meaning of life and makes them incapable of understanding truth: the living significance and the living truth are transformed into an arbitrary organization of existence whose object is the creation of human happiness in the middle of a social ants' nest.

Dostoievsky discovered that this boundless tyranny was potential in the revolutionary ideology of the left wing of the Russian *intelligentzia*, for all its apparent concern for freedom. For Dostoievsky was the first to see things no others had seen and always he saw further ahead than anyone else. He knew that the revolution which he could perceive in the underground currents of the Russia of his day would not lead to freedom, that bondage of the spirit was waiting for it. The astounding arguments of the *Letters from the Underworld* are further developed by Verhovensky, Shigalev, and the Grand Inquisitor; it is one and the same system throughout, and the idea that mankind would in its headstrong revolt exchange the truth of Christ for the boundless tyrannies of those three weighed upon Dostoievsky like a nightmare.

In their doctrine freedom of spirit is taken from man in the name of his own happiness; social eudaemonism is set up against liberty. If truth does not exist, then nothing is left but this compulsory organization of social happiness. The revolution would not be carried out in the name of freedom but in that of those very principles which lit the fires of the Inquisition, in the name of those "thousands of millions of children" who must be made happy. Man accepts a compulsory organization of his life because he is afraid of the burden and responsibility of freedom, but behind his renouncement there is also an excessive affirmation of freedom, of his own arbitrary will. Here again there is an ineluctable dialectic.

Just as freedom wrongly understood loses itself in tyranny, so a false equality develops into an unheard-of inequality and the despotic supremacy of a privileged minority. Dostoievsky was always of the opinion that, since they relied on an idea of absolute equality, revolutionary democracy and socialism would eventually result in the control of mankind at large by a handful of people. This is illustrated in the systems of Shigalev and of the Grand Inquisitor, and Dostoievsky, who was continually disturbed by the idea, returned to it more than once in the *Diary of a Writer*. The conclusion that he came to was that true liberty and true equality are possible only in Christ, in following the way of God-made-man. Antichrist and self-will involve tyranny; any idea of world-wide happiness and the common unity of mankind from which God is excluded means disaster for man and the loss of his freedom of spirit. Wilfulness and rebellion against that Mind which is the motive-power of the universe prevent even the idea of freedom from reaching human consciousness; freedom is ever out of the reach of a spirit not in touch with that Mind: the simply "euclidian" mind (Dostoievsky often used this expression) is unable to grasp this thing which seems to it an irrational mystery.

And the revolt of the euclidian mind against God is bound up with this misunderstanding and disowning of freedom: for if freedom does not exist as a mystery behind all creation then we can admit neither the verity of this suffering world nor of a God who could create so horrible and meaningless a thing. Under the influence of the euclidian mind man thinks he can make a better world, wherein evil and misery and the tears of the innocent shall have no part. Thence comes the logical development of the campaign against God in the name of the love of good. The world is bad, full of unfairness and injustice, therefore there cannot be a God who made it, so free man must make war on the idea of God and on the wickedness of the world. That is the latest development of the dialectic of freedom, the inner tragedy of it. From freedom in revolt arises the negation of the very idea of freedom, and it becomes impossible to find the secret of the world and of God by the light of his perfect freedom. To be able to understand this world, to keep one's faith in its deep meaning, to reconcile the existence of God with the existence of evil it is absolutely necessary that each one of us should have this irrational freedom in him, for it shows us what is the primary source of evil. The world is full of wickedness and misery precisely because it is based on freedom—

yet that freedom constitutes the whole dignity of man and of his world. Doubtless at the price of its repudiation evil and suffering could be abolished and the world forced to be "good" and "happy": but man would have lost his likeness to God, which primarily resides in his freedom.

The euclidian mind can be seen in revolt in Ivan Karamazov, and the world that he wants to create would be "good" and "happy"; but everything would be compulsorily rationalized and liberty non-existent. From its beginning it would be the prosperous social ant-heap whose enforced concord was rejected by the "gentleman with the cynical and sneering face." The euclidian mind may be able by coercive means to build up an essentially rationalized society, but there is nothing in common between that spirit and the meaning of the divine world: it is closed to it, shut up in three-dimensional space. To grasp the world's divine meaning it is necessary to penetrate into a fourth dimension: freedom is the truth of the fourth dimension, not to be had within the limits of the third, and the euclidian mind is quite incapable of resolving this problem of freedom. All Dostoievsky's characters who cultivate rebelliousness and self-will thereby reach a negation of liberty, because their consciousness is narrowed to three dimensions and other worlds are closed to them. The consequences of insurgent rationalism are deadly to human consciousness, the consequences

of insurgent revolutionism are deadly to human life:
Dostoievsky sets this out with great dialectical force.
Revolt is the child of unlimited freedom, and it ends
unavoidably in an unlimited sovereignty of necessity in thought and in unlimited tyranny in life.

That is Dostoievsky's astonishing theodicy, and it
is at the same time a justification of man. The argument everlastingly used against God is the existence
of evil in the world, and the whole of Dostoievsky's
work is an answer to that argument. I would sum it
up, in a paradoxical form, thus: *The existence of evil is
a proof of the existence of God. If the world consisted
wholly and uniquely of goodness and righteousness there
would be no need for God, for the world itself would be
god. God is, because evil is. And that means that God is
because freedom is.*

Thus does Dostoievsky arrive at the existence of
God through a consideration of the freedom of the
human spirit: those of his characters who deny this
freedom deny God, and inversely. A world in
which goodness and righteousness reign by compulsion, whose harmony is ensured by undeniable
necessity, is a godless world, a rationalized mecha-
nism, and to reject God and human liberty is to push
the world in that direction. Dostoievsky's treatment
of freedom is dynamic: he sees it continually borne
along on a dialectical movement, displaying internal
contradictions and passing through successive phases.
That is why men with static minds find it difficult to

understand his doctrine of freedom: they demand a
plain "yes" or "no" to questions that are not
patient of such an answer. Freedom is the tragic
destiny of mankind and of God, it appertains to the
very heart of being as a fundamental mystery. We
shall see that Dostoievsky's dialectic of freedom
reaches its climax in the Legend of the Grand Inquisitor, in which all problems are concentrated and all
their threads picked up and joined.

CHAPTER IV

EVIL

THE problem of evil and of wrongdoing is part and parcel of the problem of freedom. Without freedom evil is unexplainable, wherever there is freedom there is evil: if there were no freedom then God alone could be responsible for evil. Dostoievsky understood this as well as anybody, and he also understood that without freedom goodness would not exist either. The whole secret of human life and destiny depends on this notion: Freedom is irrational, and therefore it can create both good and evil. To reject freedom on the pretext that it can bring forth evil is to make the evil twice as bad, for if unconstrained good be the only good then compulsion and enforcement so far from being desirable are an aspect of Antichrist. That is the antinomy, the mystery, the riddle that Dostoievsky put before the world and went a very long way towards answering, but his conception of evil is so original that many people do not grasp it properly; one must get a clear idea of how he propounded and resolved the problem.

According to him, freedom degenerates into

arbitrary self-will, this leads to evil, and evil to criminal wrongdoing. Crime has a most important place in his work; he was, indeed, in his way, a criminologist as well as an anthropologist, for his exploration of the furthest frontiers of human nature involved him in an enquiry into the nature of crime. What is the destiny of the man who has gone beyond the limits of what is allowable? What regeneration of his being may it involve? Dostoievsky shows the ontological consequences of crime. After freedom has led through self-will to wrongdoing, punishment follows by an inner fatality, punishment which tracks man in the deepest parts of his nature. That is why Dostoievsky refused all his life to look at evil from a merely exterior point of view.

The novels and the Diary are full of criminal reports, a strange interest which is accounted for by the refusal of his spiritual nature to explain evil and wickedness by reference to social environment, an explanation which entails a denial of the expediency of punishment. He never alluded to this humani-tarian-positivist theory except with vehement dis-like: it seemed to him a denial of the depth of human nature, of the liberty of the spirit and the personal responsibility that goes with it. If man is nothing but a passive reflection of his social sur-roundings, an irresponsible creature, then there is no such thing as "man"—nor is there God, freedom, evil, or good. Such a dethronement of him who is

made but a little lower than the angels made Dostoievsky very angry, and he could not speak with
patience of this doctrine, which was widespread
even in his day. He was ready to defend the severest
penalties for crime, on the ground that they are the
more fitting to free and responsible beings. Evil
resides in the depth of human nature, in its irrational freedom, in its fall from a divine principle,
and those who favour heavy sentences may have a
more exact view of what crime is and of human
nature in general than those who deny evil on
humanitarian grounds. Dostoievsky maintained the
need of every crime being met by a punishment
that has its sanction in man's free conscience rather
than in an exterior law, and this he affirmed in the
name of the dignity and freedom of man, who cannot
agree to brand himself as irresponsible for evil and
wrongdoing, as an unfree creature, a mere passive
victim of his environment. All Dostoievsky's work is
a refutation of this slander on human nature. Evil
shows that man has an inner profundity and it is
associated with personality, which alone can create
evil and answer for it: an impersonal force cannot be
a first-mover or be responsible for anything. So we
see that Dostoievsky's notion of evil is closely con-
nected with his notion of personality and its importance. Humanitarianism denies evil because it
denies personality, and Dostoievsky combated humanitarianism in the name of mankind. If there be

such a thing as man, if there be human personality,
then evil has an inward origin and cannot be a
result of accidental circumstances brought about
by social environment; and it befits the dignity of
man and his divine sonship that he should recognize
that suffering redeems wrongdoing and quenches
evil. The idea that suffering raises man to his
highest level is essential in Dostoievsky's anthropology; suffering is the index of man's depth.

The complexity of Dostoievsky's teaching on evil
has caused some to doubt whether he were a Christian. He refused to regard it from the point of view
of law. He wished to *know* it, and to that extent was
a sort of gnostic. Evil is evil: its nature is interior
and metaphysical, not exterior and social. Man, as
a free being, is responsible for it, but it must be out-
lawed, hunted down, and destroyed, and Dostoievsky was tireless in the uprooting of it. But that was
only one aspect of his attitude. Evil is also the
tragical road that man has to tread, the destiny of
his freedom, an experience capable of enriching
and raising him. Men are free beings, living as such,
and they learn from inner experience the nothingness
of evil, how it defeats and destroys itself while it is
being experienced, and when they have purged
themselves of it they reach the light. But the truth
of this experience is a dangerous one, and it exists only
for those who are genuinely enfranchised and spiritually enlightened: it must be kept from the imma-

ture. One of the reasons why Dostoievsky may
appear a dangerous writer is that he *must* be read
only in an atmosphere of spiritual manhood. At the
same time it must be recognized that nobody has
fought against the principle of evil and the powers
of darkness more courageously than he did. But it
would have been not the slightest use to hold up a
merely legal morality before those of his characters
who had entered on the path of iniquity. Evil is
expiated in the ineluctable consequences that it
carries with it and not by any external chastisement;
all outward things are symbols of those that are
inward, and the law which strikes the transgressor
is only a symbol of his inner destiny. The torments
of a man's conscience are more frightening than the
severities of a whole code of law, and he looks at his
legal punishment as a relief from his moral torture.
There is nothing in common between the soul of
man and the law of the State, that "frozen mon-
ster." Dostoievsky showed the injustice of this sort
of law in the examination of Mitya Karamazov and
the accompanying proceedings. A human soul had
more significance for Dostoievsky than all the
empires of the world, and in that he was thoroughly
Christian. But the soul itself seeks the sword that
the State wields, and invites its punitive stroke:
punishment is a step upon its road.

Only an immature or enslaved mind would deduce

from Dostoievsky's thesis that we must choose to
follow the path of wickedness in order to enrich our
consciousness and profit from a new experience.
The theory that evil is only a moment in the evolution of good cannot be imputed to him; this evolu-
tionary optimism professed by so many theosophists
is entirely opposed to his spirit. He was no evolu-
tionist: evil for him was evil, to be burned in the fires
of hell, and that is where he cast it. He teaches
plainly that it is not a thing to be juggled with,
that it is madness to think that a man can deliberately enter on a course of wickedness to get
what he can out of it and then throw himself into the
arms of good: such an argument cannot be taken
seriously and indicates a worthless state of mind.
Certainly the tragic experience of evil can profit a
man and sharpen his understanding, certainly he
cannot thereafter return to his former stage of
development; but when a sinning man begins to
think that evil is enriching him, that it is leading to
good, that it is only a stage in his progress, from that
moment he has fallen completely: he goes all to
pieces and every door to improvement and regeneration is closed to him. Such a man can learn nothing
from his experience, he can never rise above himself:
self-satisfaction in evil is a sign of total loss. To climb
from evil to a high spiritual level one must denounce
the evil in oneself and suffer terribly, and these
sufferings Dostoievsky depicted.

Evil is essentially contradictory, and optimistically to conceive it as indispensable to the evolution of good and to try to remove its antinomy in the name of reason is to see only one aspect of it. The good that can be derived from evil is attained only by the way of suffering and repudiation of evil. Dostoievsky believed firmly in the redemptive and regenerative power of suffering: life is the expiation of sin by suffering. Freedom has opened the path of evil to man, it is a proof of freedom, and man must pay the price. The price is suffering, and by it the freedom that has been spoiled and turned into its contrary is reborn and given back to man. Therefore is Christ the Saviour freedom itself. In all Dostoievsky's novels man goes through this spiritual process, through freedom and evil to redemption. The *staretz* Zosima and Alyosha have known evil, and come through it to a higher state. Alyosha is by no means free from the troubles that arise from being a Karamazov: his brother Ivan and Grushenka both remark on it and he feels it himself; but in the mind of Dostoievsky he is the man who has emerged victorious from the test of freedom. That is how a human destiny should work out.

To speak of wrongdoing raises the question of what is allowable. Everything? It is a question that always troubled Dostoievsky, and he was always putting it in one form or another: it is behind *Crime and Punishment* and, to a considerable extent,

The Possessed and *The Brothers Karamazov*. Free man
is faced with this dilemma: Are there moral norms
and limits in my nature or may I venture to do anything? When freedom has degenerated into self-will
it recognizes nothing as sacred or forbidden, for if
there be no god but man then everything is allowable and man can try himself out at will. At the
same time he lets himself get obsessed by some fixed
idea, and under its tyranny freedom soon begins to
disappear—a process that Dostoievsky has set out
with all his power. It was the case with Raskolnikov. He does not give the impression of a free man
at all but of a maniac possessed by vicious delusions;
there is no sign of that moral independence that goes
with self-purification and self-liberation. Raskolnikov's fixed idea is to experiment with the uttermost limits of his own nature and that of mankind
in general. He regarded himself as belonging to the
pick of the world, one of those remarkable people
whose mission is to confer benefits on humanity at
large. He believed nothing to be impossible, and
was anxious to prove it in himself. Dostoievsky sim-
plified Raskolnikov's theorem by reducing it to the
terms of an elementary question: Has a very unusual
man, who is called to the service of his fellows, the
right to kill a specimen of the lowest sort of human
creature, who is only a source of evil to others, a
repulsive and aged usuress, with the sole object of
contributing to the future good of mankind? In *Crime*

and Punishment he set out most forcefully that such a thing is forbidden us and that the man who does it is spiritually lost.

All things are *not* allowable because, as immanent experience proves, human nature is created in the image of God and every man has an absolute value in himself and as such. The spiritual nature of man forbids the arbitrary killing of the least and most harmful of men: it means the loss of one's essential humanity and the dissolution of personality; it is a crime that no "idea" or "higher end" can justify. Our neighbour is more precious than an abstract notion, any human life and person is worth more here and now than some future bettering of society. That is the Christian conception, and it is Dostoievsky's. Even if he believes himself a Napoleon, or a god, the man who infringes the limits of that human nature which is made in the divine likeness falls crashing down: he discovers that he is not a superman but a weak, abject, unreliable creature—as did Raskolnikov. His experiment with his freedom and his strength had a disastrous result: instead of killing a stupid and dangerous old woman he had killed himself, and after his crime, which was an unalloyed experience, he lost his freedom and was crushed by his own powerlessness; even his pride was gone. He had learned, in fact, that it is easy to kill a man but that spiritual and not physical energy is expended in the doing of it. Nothing "great" or "marvellous,"

G—d

no world-wide echo, followed the murder, only a nothingness that overwhelmed the murderer. The divine law asserted itself, and Raskolnikov fell beneath its power. Christ came for the fulfilling of that law and not for its destruction: the freedom of the New Testament does not overturn the law of the Old but shows it in relation to a yet higher world; and it was the immutable biblical law whose force Raskolnikov felt.

Men of real genius, authentic benefactors of mankind, do not look on themselves as supermen for whom all things are lawful; on the contrary, they do great things for the world by sacrificing themselves to that which they put above man. Raskolnikov was a divided, riven being, from whom freedom was already alienated by his inner unhealthiness, whereas the truly great are integral and jealous for their own unity. Dostoievsky showed the folly of claiming to be a superman, a lying idea that is the death of man: this claim and all its cognate aspirations sooner or later collapse into a state of pitiable weakness and futility which is no longer human, and against it the true nature of religious and moral consciousness stands out with everlasting majesty. The sin and the powerlessness of man in his pretension to almightiness are revealed in sorrow and anguish; the tortured conscience of Raskolnikov is a witness not only to his transgression but also to his weakness.

The case of Raskolnikov illustrates the crisis of Humanism, what its morality leads to, the suicide of man by self-affirmation; it is played out, as the emergence of a visionary superman with a "higher" morality proves. There is no humanitarianism left in Raskolnikov, who is cruel and without pity for his neighbour: concrete, living, suffering men must be sacrificed to the idea of a superman. But Dostoievsky taught the religion of love for one's neighbour, and he denounced the falsity of this disinterestedness in favour of some far-away end out of sight and reach of mankind: there *is* a "far-away" principle, it is God—and he tells us to love our neighbour. The idea of God is the only supra-human idea that does not destroy man by reducing him to being a mere means. God reveals himself by his Son, and that Son is perfect God and perfect man, the God-man in whose perfection the divine and human are made one. Any other sort of superman debases man into an instrument, and thus the man-god kills true manhood, as can be seen in the example of Nietzsche. The Marxian ideal of an inhuman collectivism is equally deadly for mankind.

Dostoievsky studied the results of man's obsession by his own deification under several forms, individual and collective. One consequence is that there is an end to compassion, there is no more mercy. Compassion is a ray of the truth by which Christianity enlightened the world, and a renouncement of this truth completely changes one's attitude towards one's fellows. In the name of his Magnificence the Superman, in the name of the future happiness of some far-away humanity, in the name of the world-revolution, in the name of unlimited freedom for one or unlimited equality for all, for any or all of these reasons it is henceforth lawful to torture and to kill a man or any number of men, to transform all being into a means in the service of some exalted object or grand ideal. Everything is allowable when it is a question of the unbounded freedom of the superman (extreme individualism), or of the unbounded equality of all (extreme collectivism). Self-will arrogates to itself the right to decide the value of a human life and to dispose of it. The control of life and the judgment of mankind do not belong to God; man, as the depository of the "idea of the superman," takes them upon himself and his judgments are pitiless, impious and inhuman at the same time. Raskolnikov is one of the individuals possessed by this fallacious notion in whom Dostoievsky examined the progress of self-will: Raskolnikov answered the question whether or no he had the right to kill a human being in furtherance of his "idea" solely by reference to his own arbitrary will. But the answering of such a question does not belong to man but to God, who is the unique "higher idea." And he who does not bow before that higher will destroys his neighbour and destroys himself. That is the meaning of *Crime and Punishment*.

Dostoievsky examined the subject of self-will emerging into crime at greater length and in more detail in *The Possessed*, where he shows the fatal effects of the bewitchment of conscience by collectivist and individualist notions from which God is banished. Peter Verhovensky, obsessed by a false ideal, loses the likeness of man and human degradation is even more marked in him than in Raskolnikov. He is capable of anything, his "idea" would justify the vilest deeds; in his eyes man has ceased to exist and he is not a man himself—he takes us from the human world into surroundings that are outside mankind: we are suffocated. Atheistic revolutionary socialism ends definitely in the most absolute unhumanness; every criterion of good and evil is thrown aside and life is lived in an atmosphere heavy with violence and blood. The murder of Shatov, for instance, has a horrifying effect: there is something everlasting and prophetic in all this passage of *The Possessed*.

Dostoievsky was the first to see the inevitable consequences of a certain category of ideas. He saw further than Vladimir Soloviev, who made fun of the nihilists of Russia and attributed to them the formula "Men are descended from monkeys, so we must love one another!" But if we are made in the image and likeness of the monkey we shall not love but abuse and kill one another and nothing will be for-

bidden us. As for "the ideal" itself, the end which at
first appeared so noble and attractive, Dostoievsky
showed its utter degradation: it is formless, crazy,
unhuman, and under its patronage freedom is in
danger of becoming an unchecked despotism and
equality a terrifying inequality, until human nature
is destroyed in the final deification of man. Raskolnikov still had a human conscience, but in Peter
Verhovensky, one of Dostoievsky's most monstrous
types, it is completely wiped out; obsession has done
its work so well that he has become, so to say,
unable to repent. He is one of those who, according
to Dostoievsky, have no future in human destiny but
will be cut off from among men and fall into nothingness; they are no longer good seed. Such are Svidrigailov, Fyodor Pavlovitch Karamazov, Smerdyakov,
the "everlasting husband," while Raskolnikov,
Stavroguin, Kirilov, Versilov, Ivan Karamazov,
though materially lost, keep their potentiality for a
future life and a part in the destiny of mankind.

Nobody has described the torments of conscience
with quite the power of Dostoievsky, especially the
agony of repentance that a man may suffer even
though his will to wickedness has not issued in any
exterior action. Neither public opinion nor the law
of the State realizes the depth of man's latent
criminal tendencies, but man himself may know it
and hold himself deserving of the severest punish-

ment. Conscience exacts more than the frigid civil law, and in this matter is more pitiless, for it knows that we do not kill our brother only when we put a violent end to his physical life: our secret thoughts, which sometimes hardly reach our consciousness, make us murderers in spirit, and we are responsible for them. To the public eye our lives may be beyond reproach, but inwardly we are criminals, longing to take the life of this or that person among our neighbours; open crime begins in such obscure desires.

Dostoievsky shows the travail of conscience working to the point where it convicts of a crime of which no law-court would take cognizance. Ivan Karamazov did not kill his father Fyodor; it was Smerdyakov who killed him. But Ivan feels the responsibility of parricide and is crazed by the unrest of his conscience; his personality is cloven in two, his tormenting inward sin seeming to him like another self. In thought and subconsciously he had often wanted to kill his father, an ignominious and depraved creature, and his conversation was always turning to the theme that "everything is allowable." He tempted Smerdyakov and encouraged him in his wicked intention; he was the real murderer, Smerdyakov was only his other, his lower self. But neither the police nor public opinion accused or suspected Ivan: only his conscience burned his soul and choked his spirit with the fire of hell. It was false and

impious ideas that engendered the secret thoughts
by which he justified parricide, and if he is to pursue
his destiny he must needs go through the cycles of
madness and repentance. Mitya Karamazov, too.
He had not killed his father either, and he fell a victim to an unjust judgment of men. But he had said,
"Why is such a man alive?" By that exclamation he
had committed murder in the spirit, and he accepted
the undeserved penalty of the implacable civil law
in expiation of his sin.

The psychology of parricide in *The Brothers
Karamazov* has a valuable symbolical significance.
Self-will and godlessness inevitably lead man to
parricide and the negation of all sonship, and in
this way revolution is parricidal. The marvellous
delineation of the relationship between Ivan and his
"other self" illustrates how self-will and veneration
for the idea of the superman must reach a point
where man is confronted by the image of Smerdyakov; he is man's punishment, the shapeless and
deplorable caricature that results from self-deification. At the moment it is Smerdyakov who wins;
Ivan must go mad. The part played by Stavroguin
in the murder of his wife the Khromonojka (in
The Possessed) is an equally deep demonstration of
the secret presence of criminality in man's heart,
whence it may be manifested only with his tacit
permission. Fedka Katorjnik, the murderer, maintains that Stavroguin has led him on and that he was

only his agent, and Stavroguin himself recognizes that he is guilty.

"Neither a man nor a nation can live without a 'higher idea,' and there is only one such idea on this earth, that of an immortal human soul; all the other 'higher ideas' by which men live flow from that. . . . Following on the loss of the idea of immortality, suicide appears a complete and ineluctable necessity for every man who is in the slightest degree above the level of the beasts of the field. . . . The idea of immortality is life itself, the definitive formulation and the first source of the truth and integrity of conscience." Thus does Dostoievsky speak of immortality in the *Diary of a Writer*. It was a basic idea of his that if there be no immortality then everything is lawful for us, and immortality accordingly enters into the problem of evil and wrongdoing. How are we to understand this bond between them? We need not, anyhow, suppose that Dostoievsky looked at the question from the over-simple and utilitarian point-of-view that in eternal life evil will be punished and goodness rewarded: that was too elementary a way for him to put it. As he understood it, it is inasmuch as he is an immortal creature that man has an absolute value and cannot allow himself to be used as a means or instrument of any "interest" whatsoever: the denial of man's immortality is equivalent to a denial of man. Either he is an immortal spirit who carries an eternal destiny or else he is only an empi-

rical and ephemeral phenomenon, the passive product of his natural and social surroundings. If the
last be the case, he has no intrinsic value, and evil
and sin do not exist. Therefore Dostoievsky de-
fended man's immortal soul, a free and responsible
soul whose last end is everlasting and absolute. To
accept the existence of moral evil and man's responsibility for it is to recognize the very essence of
human personality: evil is associated with personality and egocentricity. But that personality is
immortal, and to destroy the eternal personal principle constitutes evil, while its affirmation constitutes good. Therefore to deny immortality is to
deny the existence both of good and evil. If man is
not a free, immortal, personal being he may do
anything, he is responsible for nothing, he has no
intrinsic value. This notion of the absolute value
of each individual lies at the heart of Dostoievsky's
moral theory. The life and destiny of the least of
human beings has an absolute meaning in respect
of eternity: his life and his destiny are everlasting.
For that reason one may not do away with a single
human creature and escape punishment; we must
consider the divine image and likeness in every one,
from the most noble to the most despicable. That is
Dostoievsky's ethical teaching. It is not only that
which is "far away," the "higher idea," or unusual
people like Raskolnikov and Stavroguin and Ivan
Karamazov that have intrinsic value, but also our

ordinary neighbour, the Marmeladovs, the Lebiad-
kins, the Sniguirevs, the horrible old usuress. The
man who kills another kills himself and denies the
immortality and everlastingness of both. This
unanswerable dialectic is purely Christian. Man
should avoid sin not alone from a utilitarian fear of
punishment but primarily because sin gives the lie
to his own eternal nature, that nature of which our
conscience is the expression.

Dostoievsky envisaged suffering from two sides,
and this duality, which is at first difficult to grasp,
explains the contradictory judgments which re-
spectively find him the most compassionate and the
most heartless of writers. The truth is that his work
is permeated by an infinite compassion for man and
everywhere teaches pity and charity. No one has felt
human suffering more acutely than Dostoievsky, and
his heart is ever bleeding. He experienced penal
servitude and lived for years among convicts, and he
never ceased to pray to God for mankind. The
sufferings of innocent children upset him and hurt
his conscience more than anything else, and the justification of their tears was for him the task of all
theodicy: he understood the common repulsion of a
universal order the price of whose establishment
seems to be the misery of the innocent. Ivan Karamazov challenges his brother: "Suppose that you
are building up a fabric of human destiny with the

object of making people happy at last and giving
them peace and rest, but that in order to do so it is
necessary and unavoidable to torture a single tiny
baby . . . and to found your building on its tears—
would you agree to undertake the building on that
condition?"   "No, I wouldn't agree," answers
Alyosha, and Fyodor Dostoievsky spoke through
his mouth. All his life he was asking, in the words of
Mitya, "Why are there these fathers of families
ruined by a fire? Why are there all these poor people,
this crying baby? Why the barren *steppe*? Why don't
they all hug and kiss and sing gaily together? Why
are they grey with wretchedness? Why don't they
feed the baby?"

Nevertheless, Dostoievsky was very far from being
a sloppy sentimentalist. If he preached pity he also
preached suffering, the suffering that is deserved and
comes to man from his misused freedom. We have
seen that he would not hear of buying immunity
from suffering at the price of freedom: he urged
people to accept the one as an inevitable consequence of the other. Dostoievsky's "cruelty" is an
aspect of his thoroughgoing acceptance of liberty;
the words of the Grand Inquisitor might have been
spoken to him: "Thou didst choose all that is unusual,
vague, and puzzling, things beyond the strength of
men, and thus thou didst act as if thou didst not
love them." Now the unusual, the vague, and the
puzzling are linked with man's irrational freedom.

Dostoievsky saw that suffering is a sign of a greater dignity, the mark of a free creature. Suffering is a result of evil, but evil is not worn down by suffering alone. Dostoievsky's heroes pass through hell and they reach the outer gates of paradise—which are less easily seen than hell.

By the way of freedom man comes to evil and it is in evil that he reaches that state of inner division, the results of Dostoievsky's searches into which are of such interest to psychologists and psychiatrists— things are more quickly and clearly revealed to a great artist than to the experts. Unrestrained and objectless freedom, deprived of God and his grace and degenerating into self-will, ceases to be capable of making a choice and is bandied about in opposite directions. Then is the time that two selves appear in a man and his personality is cloven apart. Raskolnikov and Stavroguin, Versilov and Ivan Karamazov, all have lost personal integrity in this way and lead in many respects a double life. In extreme cases the other self separates from the man and is personified apart, a symbol of inner evil—the Devil. Dostoievsky showed this phase most forcefully in that nightmare of Ivan Karamazov, his interview with Satan, where Ivan tells him: "You are an incarnation of myself, but of only one side of me—of my thoughts and feelings, and only of the nastiest and stupidest of them. . . . You are myself, myself—but with a different face. . . . You are not someone else;

you are I, and nothing more. You are nothing—
only my own fancy." Dostoievsky's Satan is not a
handsome and impressive demon who appears
"with fiery wings, thundering and lightening in a
crimson cloud," but a middle-aged and rather
vulgar person with a suburban mind, whose ambition is to take flesh as "a well-fed shopkeeper who
weighs fifteen stone": he is an empty spirit. Common sense forbids him to assume the appearance of
Christ, and as Ivan's "euclidian mind" is closely
related to common sense his arguments are very like
those of Satan himself.

All Dostoievsky's "divided" people have a devil,
though less clearly visible than Ivan's is to him.
This second self is the spirit of not-being, it represents the loss of the essence of personality and is the
manifestation of an empty liberty, the freedom of
nothingness. The ideal of Sodom is only a ghost of
life, and Svidrigailov, definitely given up to that
ideal, himself becomes nothing more than a phantom
with no vestige of personality left. Nothingness is
immanent in evil. The divided man can find salvation nowhere but in the second, final, freedom,
freedom in the grace and truth of Christ. To mend
that inner cleavage and banish that nightmare of
Satan a man must make a definitive choice, and
choose Being itself.

CHAPTER V

LOVE

DOSTOIEVSKY laid bare the sensual element in the complex Russian nature and his plots are worked out in a stormy atmosphere of passion: there is nothing like it in any other Russian writer. He discovered among the educated classes the same obscure ethnical tendency that showed itself in the mass of the people through the mystical sect of the *Khlisty.** It was a dionysiac movement and for Dostoievsky love is exclusively dionysian, tearing the individual to pieces. It is volcanic, an explosion of all the forces of passion pent up in men; it knows neither law nor form and its pressure drives the deepest parts of human nature to the surface. Dostoievsky's dynamism is nowhere more marked than here: love is a leaping flame, a devouring fire—but a fire that can be turned to ice. Love simply wears out some of Dostoievsky's men and reduces them to frigid insensibility; they become extinct volcanoes.

* A mystical Russian sect, possibly deriving from the Bogomili. Their Christology is adoptionist, and their religious dances are not unlike those of the Dervishes. They have been accused of wholesale debauchery, which is, however, denied by the Rev. F. Conybear in his *Russian Dissenters*. TR.

Russian literature knows nothing of the lofty types of love that have been conceived in western Europe; it has nothing to show like the love sung by the troubadours, no Tristan and Iseult, no Dante and Beatrice, no Romeo and Juliet. The common bond between two human beings, the love-cult of woman, is a beautiful flower sprung from European Christian culture, and Russia had no age of chivalry with its garden of *trouvères*. This irreparable spiritual lack gives a flavour of affliction and pain, of melancholy and often of distortion, to all Russian manifestations of love. There has been no real romanticizing of love in Russia, for Romanticism is a purely Western phenomenon.

The place that love holds in Dostoievsky's novels is a very big one but it is not an independent place: love has no value in itself or symbolism of its own but serves only to show man his tragic road and to be a reagent of his freedom. Consequently it plays a very different part from that assigned to it by, say, Pushkin in the case of Tatiana and by Tolstoy in *Anna Karenina*, and the feminine element itself is conceived differently. Woman never appears as an independent being for, as we shall see, Dostoievsky was interested in her solely as a milestone on the road of man's destiny. His anthropology is masculine: the soul is primarily the masculine principle in mankind and the feminine principle is the inward theme of man's tragedy, his temptation. Dostoievsky

has given us such representations of love as that of
Muishkin and Rogojin for Nastasia Philippovna, of
Mitya Karamazov for Grushenka, of Versilov for
Katerina Nicolaevna, of Stavroguin for many
women—not a great woman among them, not a
single female type with any value of her own. It is
always man who is tortured by a tragic destiny, of
which woman is only the interior expression.

Dostoievsky reveals the hopeless tragedy of love,
the human impossibility of realizing it in the ordinary conditions of life. Love seemed murderous to
him, as it did to the poet Tiutshev:

> "We love in a death-dealing way,
>   for in the rushing blindness of our passion
>   we do most surely kill
>   our heart's most dear delight."

Dostoievsky shows neither the delectation of
passion nor the beauty proper to family life nor that
supreme love which achieves a total oneing and
fusion. The mystery of marriage is not consummated.
He takes an individual at the exact moment in his
history when the foundations of his life are undermined, and love serves only as an index of his inner
division. It is a highly dynamic element, it calls
down lightning and stirs up tumult but it is never an
end in itself. Nothing is gained by love; it is simply a
tornado that bears man on to shipwreck. Why?

H—d

Because it is a manifestation of self-will and as such breaks up the human person and cleaves it in twain.

Here we reach another of Dostoievsky's essential points in the destiny of man and his freedom. Love is just a moment in that destiny. Human destiny, I say, and it is the destiny of Raskolnikov, Stavroguin, Kirilov, Muishkin, Versilov, of Dmitry, Ivan, and Alyosha Karamazov—but not of Nastasia Philippovna, Aglae, Lisa, Elisaveta Nicolaevna, Grushenka, and Katerina Nicolaevna. Once again, woman is a stumbling-block in the way of male destiny, and it is a waste of time to look for any "cult of the eternal feminine" in the work of Dostoievsky. His special reverence for mother-earth and for our Lady had nothing to do with his representations of love or the feminine forms in his imagination. In the character of Maria Timofeevna, "the Limper," alone does he seem to have attempted to show something intrinsic, but this has been exaggerated and he was much less interested in her than in Stavroguin. Anyway, he never worked out a female character as Tolstoy did Anna Karenina or Natasha; Anna has her own proper life and is the principal figure of the book, whereas Nastasia Philippovna and Grushenka are no more than strong influences in the lives of the men who meet them. Dostoievsky could never live with his "heroines" as Tolstoy did with his: he is concerned with them only in reference to his men, as agents of their temptation and disturbance. Woman's daemonic nature interests him inasmuch as it stirs up a passion which produces division of personality in man. Dostoievsky's men remain shut up in themselves without any escape towards another being, a woman: the drama of passion is played within them and the woman concerned is only an item in what may be called the drawing-up of an interior balance-sheet.

Since he found human destiny to reside in the destiny of personality and this personal element to be developed predominantly among men, Dostoievsky could not illustrate the course of personality by the history of a woman's soul. Man is fettered to woman by passionate desire, but this passion remains, if I may put it so, a matter between him and himself, an affair of his own temperament: it can never unite him with the desired woman. Perhaps Dostoievsky always shows feminine nature as broken and ailing because it seemed to him to carry the load of this everlasting separation from man. He maintained that love is a tragedy from which there is no way out. And, unlike the mystic Jacob Boehme and others, he did not believe that the final expression of human nature is androgynous. What he tried to make clear was that woman represents man's destiny; for himself he remained estranged from feminine nature and emphasized the duality so far as possible. Dostoievsky's human being was not androgynous, he was male.

Dostoievsky leads the individual through the tortuous windings of his divided personality, a division of which woman is the incarnation. For him sexual love signifies the loss of the integrity of human nature and that is why he finds passion unclean, for pureness is realized only in unity: debauchery is disaggregation. Love is decomposed into two elements, and to make them more perceptible a lover nearly always loves two objects at the same time, a duality that Dostoievsky describes with incomparable power. He reveals two principles in love, two gulfs in which the individual is swallowed up, sensuality and pity,* and he shows love welling from both these exaltations and tending always to extremes. That is what interested him—he would have found a "moderate" love worthless. What he wanted to do was to conduct experiments on human nature and to demonstrate its depth by showing people in exceptional circumstances. Dostoievsky's love is divided, and the loved one is divided too: there is no unity or perfection in it. And it cannot be otherwise in this realm of self-will, where human nature is torn between contraries and runs the risk of losing its own image as a result. The two terms of the division in love, sensuality and pity, know no measure, obey no higher principle, and their scorch-

---

* The primary meaning of the Russian word *zhalost* (or *jalost*) is "pity." Here it is used in a very common sense (especially in the popular language) to mean a mixture of love, pity, and protectiveness, somewhat the feeling of a parent for his helpless child. Tr.

ing power reduces the individual to ashes. Dostoievsky detected a sort of sensuality even in pity. It is the divided man, not he who has preserved his integrity, that passion deranges, and it supplies no means of overcoming his delirious disunity; man brings his own dividedness to love, and love in its turn aggravates it. A man can never regain his unity and integrity by way of this love, whether through infinite sensuality or infinite pity; he will never arrive at communion with the loved one in whom his being can again be made whole. He remains alone, the plaything of his exhausting antinomian passions.

It is easy to understand that love as Dostoievsky conceived it is nearly always daemonic, begetting obsession and a state of white-hot excitement: it is not only the lovers who go mad, all around them are infected as well. The love of Versilov for Katerina Nicolaevna, of Muishkin and of Rogojin for Nastasia Philippovna and Aglae create a frenzied atmosphere that produces over-tension everywhere, Stavroguin and Lisa stir up a very hubbub of hell, the loves of Mitya and Ivan Karamazov and Grushenka and Katerina Ivanovna are a cause of crime and madness. Never in any degree does this love find rest, never does it lead to the joy of complete union, there is no light in it; on the contrary, it is always gloomy and destructive, a vision of unhappiness and pain. I have pointed out above that for Dostoievsky love serves to widen man's inner division rather than to heal it. He always has two women, symbolizing the two streams of passion, who make of their love the starting-point of a pitiless struggle in which each ruins herself in destroying the other. In *The Idiot* it is Nastasia Philippovna and Aglae who thus confront one another, in *The Brothers Karamazov* it is Grushenka and Katerina Ivanovna, and there is something quite merciless in the rivalries of these women. The same thing occurs in *The Possessed* and in *A Raw Youth*, though in a less open way. Man's nature is divided, woman's is as yet dark: she is a sort of pit for man to stumble into— there is no longer any trace in her of the blessed Mother of God.

The blame is man's and his alone. It is he who has departed from the feminine principle, who has renounced his mother-earth, his proper virginity— that is to say, his integrity—to follow the road of falsehood and division. Now he is powerless before the feminine principle, as we see over and over again in the novels, in Stavroguin, Versilov and the rest. Men and women live in a tragical state of separation, a source of torment and distress to one another. The man has not the strength to dominate the woman; he does not understand her nature and sees it only cross his path as the incarnation of his own division.

The theme of a double love, so common in Dos-

toievsky, can be best examined in *The Idiot*, where
Muishkin loves Nastasia Philippovna and Aglae at
the same time. Muishkin is an uncorrupted,
angelical creature, free from the common appetite
for sensuality, but for all that his is a diseased and
divided love, doomed to sterility. The division is
within himself, in the collision of two contrary principles. He is not able to join himself either to Nastasia or to Aglae, he is essentially unsuited to marriage and wedded love; Aglae's beauty enthralls
him and he is ready to serve her as a "faithful
knight." But if Dostoievsky's other heroes suffer
from too much sensuality Muishkin suffers from
being without it altogether; he has not got the sen-
sibility of a healthy man, his love is without flesh and
blood, and accordingly the other pole, pity, is all the
more strongly developed. He loves Nastasia Philippovna with an excessive compassion that is itself
destructive, for it is a demonstration of his self-will
transgressing in degree what is allowable to man: he
is swallowed up and lost in the gulf of his own pity.
This one-sided feeling is a product of the relative
conditions obtaining in this world, but Muishkin
wants to exalt it into eternity and impose it on God.
Because of Nastasia and his pity for her he forgets his
duty to himself; he does not realize fulness of life in
it, he does not even give himself up to it entirely, for
he is divided within—he is loving Aglae in a very
different way all the time.

Here Dostoievsky shows how an unhealthy passion can get hold of and possess a good, a seraphic man to his ruin. In Muishkin's love there is no impulse towards total union with a single and sufficient creature: this huge destructive pity can only be evoked in relation to one with whom union is impossible. Under its searing trials Muishkin's nature too shows its dionysism, of a particular kind, quiet and Christian; he is always being lost in ecstatic silence, like a sort of angelic rapture. Perhaps all his troubles are due to the fact that he is too much like the angels, unfitted for human conditions and not wholly a man—he certainly cannot be classed among those in whom Dostoievsky illustrated masculinity. In Alyosha he posited an accomplished being, knowing the world and experiencing human passions, who overcomes his inner division and escapes towards the light (incidentally, he is not one of the best drawn of Dostoievsky's characters); Muishkin, on the other hand, is an unearthly figure without its full complement of human attributes and cannot be considered as explaining any aspect of the human tragedy at all—he puts his love on the eternal plane and the story is more concerned with his supernatural aspect. Dostoievsky endowed Muishkin with an astonishing gift of divination. He foretells what will happen to those among whom he lives, reads the souls of the women whom he loves, and prophetically reconciles the notions of a temporal and of a supernatural world. This fore-knowledge is the only hold he has over women; he cannot either dominate them or be joined as one with them.

Dostoievsky's women excite either desire or pity, and some of them arouse the different emotions in different men. Nastasia Philippovna is a source of endless compassion to Muishkin and of avid craving to Rogojin; Sonia, mother of the "raw youth," awakes pity and Grushenka desire; the relationship of Versilov and Katerina Nicolaevna is sensual, but he loves his wife with pity; there is a bond of the senses between Stavroguin and Lisa, but in a weakened form, repressed, as it were. Neither the strength of sensuality nor of pity can alone unite the lover to the beloved; both have their part in the secret of loving intercourse, but it resides in neither to the exclusion of the other. As for loving intercourse itself, the bridal gift, Dostoievsky did not know it: he did not understand the fusion of two souls into one, the making of two bodies one, and that is why for him love is doomed to disaster from the very beginning.

The interpretation of love given in *A Raw Youth* is especially interesting. Versilov's love for Katerina Nicolaevna is "divided" and springs from the division in his personality: he loves her with desire, Sonia with pity. And this love is not a means for

him to escape from his "I" and find unity in
"another self" but a private concern of Versilov
with himself, an account to be kept between him and
his own destiny. Versilov puzzles everybody: there
is a secret in his life. In *A Raw Youth*, as well as in
The Possessed and several other books, Dostoievsky's
literary method is to begin the action at a point
after the life of the chief character has been marked
by some happening of special importance which
will have an influence on a long chain of events; in
the case of Versilov this took place long ago, abroad,
and we are shown its results. Women play a big
part, he is regarded as "a prophet of women," but
he is no less unfitted for wedded love than Stavroguin himself: indeed, he is nearly akin to him, a
chastened and fully mature Stavroguin. Out-
wardly he appears calm, almost indifferent to everything, but behind this tranquil mask there are lively
passions, and his love, powerless ever to achieve
anything and hidden though it be, is a source of disturbance to all around him. Here, as always with
Dostoievsky, a man's inward disposition, though not
even openly declared, infects his environment. It is
only towards the finish that Versilov's passion breaks
out, and then he indulges in a succession of crazy
actions that betray the disorder of his inner life. His
meeting and explanation with Katerina at the end of
the book is a most remarkable representation of
passionate love. The volcano was not quite extinct

after all, and the boiling lava that was so near the surface and caused the sultry atmosphere throughout the book blows up at last. "I will ruin you!" he shouts at her, in a final revelation of the daemoniac element in his hopeless love; he is never to know the hidden mysteries of union, the man shall remain everlastingly separated from the woman. Not that Katerina Nicolaevna did not return Versilov's love, she did. But their love is without hope of any fruitful issue because of the impenetrability of masculine nature, its inner division and its incapacity to escape into another "self." The mighty personality of Stavroguin declines and is lost from exactly the same cause.

The debauchery which so often results from sensuality is according to Dostoievsky a phenomenon of the metaphysical and not of the physical order. Self-will begets inner division, which in turn begets debauchery wherein the unity of human personality is lost. In the divided, dismembered, depraved man, shut up in himself, ability to join with another creature is dead; his own self begins to break up; he no longer seeks in love another being different from himself, but just seeks love. Real love is what one bears towards another; debauchery is love and affirmation of self, conducing to the ruin of self. Human personality is strengthened by communion with its kind; debauchery is the most frozen isolation to which a man can condemn himself, a decline to a

sentient nothingness. Delight of the senses is as it
were a stream of fire, but when it deteriorates into
lechery the fire goes out and passion becomes as
cold as ice. Dostoievsky showed this process very
powerfully in the person of Svidrigailov, where we
see the ontological degeneration of a human personality and its destruction by an unbridled sensuality that ends in frantic debauchery; Svidrigailov
comes to pertain to an illusory world of not-being,
with something unhuman about him. Self-will and
self-sufficiency always beget depravity. There is still
a certain warmth and humanness about the sensuality of Mitya Karamazov: the Karamazovs'
lechery has not yet reached the region of ice that is
one of the circles of Dante's hell. But Stavroguin's
has. His tragedy is that of a distinguished and
unusually gifted man who wastes himself in arbitrary, unruly, and uncontrolled follies; he gives way
to his caprices till he has no power of discrimination
left. The words addressed to Dasha in a letter that
she finds after his death have an agonized ring: "I've
tried my strength everywhere . . . Whenever I have
tested it, whether for my own satisfaction or because
I wanted to show off, I have found it limitless, as I
still do. . . . But what I never have seen and don't
see now is what to apply my strength to . . . I am
still capable, as I always was, of wanting to do
something good and finding satisfaction in it. . . .
I've tried debauchery on a large scale and wasted

my strength on it, but I don't like vice and I didn't
want it. . . . I can never abdicate my judgment or
believe in an idea to such a degree as he [Kirilov]
did. I can't even be interested in ideas to that
extent."

Good and evil, our Lady and Sodom, were equally
attractive to Stavroguin, and this inability to make a
choice is the exact indication of the alienation of
freedom and loss of personality that are involved
in self-will and inner division. We learn from the
example of Stavroguin that to want everything,
without distinction and careless of the limits of our
human nature, is equivalent to wanting nothing at
all, and that an unmeasurable strength directed
towards no end is no better than complete weakness.
Stavroguin's malignant and aimless eroticism ended
in a veritable sexual impotence: he became absolutely incapable of loving a woman. Inner division
wears away personality, and this division can be
overcome only by making a choice, by selecting a
definite object for one's love, whether it be God as
against Satan, the image of our Lady as against
Sodom, or one particular woman as against the
unnumbered all other women. Debauchery means
the absolute inability to choose from among many
attractions; it results from the alienation of freedom
and the will's balance, from the fall into nothingness
that is the penalty of not having the courage necessary to maintain the reality of one's being. Debau-

chery is man's line of least resistance, and it is right to envisage it primarily from the ontological rather than from the moral point of view. That is what Dostoievsky did.

Sensuality is the Karamazovs' kingdom: not that sensuality concentrated in one special object that is a part of all real love, but a diffused, vicious sensuality which embodies the idea of evil. Alyosha alone among them was able to save his personality, and this he did through Christ—left to his own resources man can do nothing. Old Fyodor Pavlovitch Karamazov has lost any possibility of free choice once and for all. He is possessed and controlled entirely by the feminine principle in one or other of its innumerable incarnations, no female is too repulsive or ill-favoured in his eyes: Elisaveta Smerdiashchaia is just a woman to him. . . .

At this stage the element of individuality has definitely disappeared, but the debauchery that kills personality is not a first principle: it supposes a previous radical alteration in the personality concerned and is an expression of a disaggregation that has already begun under the influence of self-will and self-affirmation. In order to keep these man must necessarily humble himself before a principle that is above his own "I". Personality is bound up with love, but it is a love that goes out towards fellowship with another being. The love that does not get beyond self brings forth vice, and it is useless to turn

to the other pole of love, pity: pity can save nobody
from the demon of sensuality, for it is itself sensual, an
incomplete feeling, a mutilated piece of divided love
without the impulse towards another which is needed
for the recovery towards a whole personality. Certainly sensuality and compassion are the two everlasting elements without which there can be no love,
both of them indulged in moderation and justified by
the beauty of the beloved; and above all they must be
irradiated by seeing the dear face in the light of God
and associating together in his presence. That is in
truth love. But Dostoievsky does not show us a
happy realization of it: Alyosha and Lisa are the only
couple he conceived in a cheerful spirit, and they are
hardly satisfying. It is not much use to look in his
work for the ideal of the good and of our Lady; his
achievement was to make an impressive contribution
to the study of the tragic side of love.

Dostoievsky understood Christianity as the religion
of love that it is, and the voice of St. John is heard in
the teaching of the *staretz* Zosima and in the other
religious reflections scattered throughout his works;
he saw the "Russian Christ" in the first place as the
messenger of unbounded love. But he found that the
tragic antinomy which he revealed in sexual love is
present also in social love: man's love for his neighbour and for mankind can be impious and completely foreign to Christianity. In the striking picture

of the future that he puts into the mouth of Versilov
(in *A Raw Youth*) all people love each other and are
at one because the great idea of God and eternal life
which used to sustain them has now been lost.

"I suppose the struggle to be over," says Versilov
to the young man. "There is quiet again after the
curses and the hissing and the mud; men are left
alone as they desired, the great idea of the past is gone
from them; the mighty disposer of power from whom
they drew their food and warmth for so long has
disappeared like the sun at evening in the pictures of
Claude Lorrain: one would think that it is the last
day of mankind. All of a sudden men realize that
they are alone, they feel as though they were orphans.
My dear boy, I have never been able to imagine men
as boorish and ungrateful. When they are deserted
they will stand together more closely and more
affectionately, they will hold each other's hands in
the knowledge that henceforward they together
represent the whole universe. For to fill the place of
the lost great idea of immortality men will give to the
world, to nature, to their neighbours, to every blade
of grass, that overflowing love which they formerly
consecrated to the vision of eternal life. So frenziedly
will they cherish the earth and its life that gradually
they will grow accustomed to seeing in it their beginning and end, and they will cherish it with a special
affection, no longer the same as before. They will
explore the phenomena of nature and discover un-

expected secrets in her, for they will be looking at the
world with new eyes, as a lover looks at his mistress.
They will come to themselves and hasten to embrace
one another, knowing that their days are numbered
and that there is nothing else. They will work for one
another, each giving his earnings to all and being only
too glad to do so. Every child will know that he can
find a father or mother in any human creature—for
every man and woman will think as he watches the
setting sun: To-morrow may be my last day; but
what matter?—There will be others here when I am
gone, and after them their children. So they will be
supported, not by the hope of a meeting beyond the
grave, but by the thought that others will replace
them on earth who will always love and tremble for
one another. They will turn quickly to love to stifle
the sorrow that will be deep down in their hearts.
They will be bold and fearless for themselves but
nervous for others, each fearful for the safety and
happiness of his neighbour. They will be mutually
affectionate without embarrassment and as endearing
together as children; when they meet they will regard
each other with a searching and meaningful look, a
look filled with both love and sadness."

In this remarkable passage Versilov draws a
picture of that love without God which is the antithesis of Christian love, a love which does not come
from the essence of Being but from a contempt of
being, which is not an affirmation of everlasting life

I—d

but a making-the-most of the passing hour of earthly
existence. It is nothing but a fantastic illusion; mankind without God can know no such love but rather
will achieve the kind described in *The Possessed*. But
Versilov's utopia, such as it is, is interesting in that
it develops Dostoievsky's ideas about love. A godless
mankind must end in savagery and massacre, bringing man down to the level of a mere means. If a man
loves his neighbour in God, that love strengthens his
notions of eternity: it is the only real love, Christian
love, linked to the soul's immortality, an affirmation
of it. True love is bound up with personality, and
personality with immortality: that is Dostoievsky's
essential idea and it is as valid for love between the
sexes as for any other kind of human affection.

There is the other love, which is directed to man
apart from God, which disowns the eternal aspect of
man (perceptible only in God), which in a word is
not turned towards everlasting life. This love is
impersonal and collective, it drives people to huddle
together so that they may not be so frightened of
living, for in losing faith in God and immortality
they have lost the meaning of life. That sort of love
is the final term of self-will and self-affirmation; God
having no place in it, man denies his own spiritual
nature and its primacy and is a traitor to freedom and
immortality. The last refuge for man's "idealism" is
in the pity he feels for his fellows as feeble creatures
who are the plaything of blind necessity; beyond

that, ideas cease to exist and reason itself is abolished. But this pity is not the same as Christian compassion. In the Christian conception of love, all men are brothers in Christ, and love in Christ is the recognition of the divine sonship of each and every individual, made in God's image and likeness. Man's greatest duty is to love God: that is the first commandment. The second is to love his neighbour. And it is possible for two creatures to love one another only because God exists and is their common Father—it is the divine image and likeness that is lovable in our fellow-men. If there be no God, to love man means to deify him, to revere him as an absolute—hence the dangerous notion of the man-god which lies in wait for us to enslave and devour the individual. It is indeed impossible to love man apart from God, and for that very reason Ivan Karamazov declares that he cannot love his fellows. Outside of the Christian conception love is an illusion and a lie. The idea of the superman, deified man, is fatal to mankind: the contrary idea, of God tabernacling with men, becoming himself a man, is the only reliable one, strengthening him for eternal life.

Godliness and un-Christian love is the principal theme of the Legend of the Grand Inquisitor, and I shall come back to it. Dostoievsky several times tackled the subject of the denial of God in the name of social eudaemonism, of humanitarianism, of man's happiness during his short earthly sojourn, and each time he declared the necessity of union between love and freedom. He saw that this union is realized only in Christ. Man's love for woman, man's love for his neighbour, becomes impious directly he is deprived of spiritual freedom and directly his vision of immortality and eternity is dimmed. Real love is the affirmation of eternity.

CHAPTER VI

REVOLUTION. SOCIALISM

THE underground revolution in the spirit of man began in the epoch of which Dostoievsky was the delineator and philosopher. On the surface nothing seemed changed. The old way of life tried for the last time under Alexander III to consolidate itself and managed to produce an appearance of general well-being, but underneath things were moving tumultuously. Neither the theorists nor men-of-action who were directing this movement had a full understanding of what was going on; they had not made it, but rather it had made them. Without doubt they were active enough so far as exterior motion was concerned, but in matters of the spirit they were passive and let themselves be carried along on the stream.

Dostoievsky, with the foresight of genius, perceived the character and ideological bases of the Russian—and perhaps universal—revolution that was in preparation. In the most exact sense of the word, he was the prophet of the revolution: it took place in the way he said it would; he revealed its inner dialectic and gave it a form, grasping its nature in

133

the depth of the spirit's evolution and not from the
outward circumstances that composed the empirical
reality around him. *The Possessed* was not a novel
about the present but about the future. There was
not yet a Stavroguin or a Kirilov or a Shatov or a
Peter Verhovensky or a Shigalev in the Russia of the
'sixties and 'seventies; such types came later, in the
twentieth century, when the human soul had
become more complex and religious inspirations had
passed over the land. The Netchaev affair,* which
suggested the plot of *The Possessed*, did not actually
resemble the book at all, for Dostoievsky was not
interested in surface things: inner depths and final
principles were his concern. Now these must be
sought in the process of becoming, and Dostoievsky
kept his whole attention fixed on that which was to
be, the goal which the turbulent inner movement
was bound to reach. An artistic talent such as his
may be considered to have a prophetical character
of itself.

Like his attitude towards evil, Dostoievsky's view
of revolution involves an antinomy. No one has
denounced more strongly than he the falsehood and

* Netchaev was a young school-teacher who conspired against the
government. He worked in the name of a non-existent committee
and organized several small groups of which he was in full control.
He was dictatorial and unscrupulous and eventually ordered the
murder of one of the conspirators, which brought the whole thing to
light. In 1871 eighty-seven people were tried: thirty-seven were
sentenced to imprisonment, the rest were exiled by administrative
order. TR.

unrighteousness that make revolutions; he saw in them a mighty spirit of Antichrist, the ambition to make a god of man. But he must not be regarded as a conservative or a reactionary in the current sense: he was revolutionary-minded in a deeper way. He saw no possibility of a return to the conception of life, a static and immovable form, that existed before the arising of the revolutionary spirit. His mind was too apocalyptic to imagine any such restoration of a former tranquillity. He was the first to notice how movements gain impetus in the world, the whole tending towards an end. "The end of the world is coming," he wrote in his notebook. That is not the attitude of a conservative. His hostility against revolution was not that of a man with a stale mind who takes some interest or other in the old social organization, but the hostility of an apocalyptic being who takes the side of Christ in his supreme struggle with Antichrist. Now he who marches with Christ with his face towards the last great battle at the end of time is a man of the future and not of the past, every bit as much as him who marches with Antichrist and fights in his ranks at the last day. Generally speaking, the conflict between revolutionaries and counter-revolutionaries is a superficial affair, an opposition of interests: on the one side, the "has-beens" who have been supplanted, on the other, the supplanters who now have the first places at feasts. Dostoievsky stood aside from that contest for the favours of this world, as have almost all the great men, who cannot be definitely assigned to one camp or the other. Can it be said, for example, that Carlyle or Nietzsche was either "revolutionary" or "counter-revolutionary"? Probably from the point of view of the demagogues they must be ranged, like Dostoievsky himself, among the counter-revolutionaries, for the reason that all spirit must be at enmity with anything which *prima facie* deserves the name of revolution, and because, in general, revolution of the spirit opposes the spirit of revolution. Dostoievsky was very much this apocalyptic man, and the usual standards of revolutionary and counter-revolutionary cannot be applied to him. For him revolution was as near as may be a reaction.

We have seen that Dostoievsky shows that when freedom deteriorates into self-will it must lead to revolt and revolution, by a fatal destiny of men who have repudiated their divine origins. Revolution is not conditioned by outward causes and circumstances but is determined interiorly: it is an indication of a disastrous alteration of man's original relationship with God, with the world, and with his fellows. Dostoievsky studied the paths along which they are borne to revolution and made its dialectic clear: it is an anthropological study of the limits of human nature and of the ways of human life. What he found in the destinies of individuals he found also in the destinies of peoples; the question whether

' 'everything is allowable" is put before society at large as well as to particular men, and the same roads that lead an individual to crime lead society to revolution. Individuals and peoples who have equally exceeded their respective limits are equally deprived of freedom. Dostoievsky foresaw the fatal process that in a revolution leads to loss of liberty in unbelievable slavery and prophesied even the details of its windings. He did not like revolution for this very reason, that it leads man into bondage and the loss of his freedom of spirit; he denounced its fundamental principles because they must result in enslavement, the negation of equality and brotherhood among men. He demonstrated the deceptions of revolution, that it can never give what it promises: it puts Antichrist in the place of Christ, and the same men who have refused freely to be one with our Lord allow themselves to be forced into unity with the opposite spirit.

The nature of "the revolution" was for Dostoievsky primarily a question of socialism. The problem which socialism presents was always in the forefront of his preoccupations, and some of the most searching things that have ever been said about it emanated from him. He understood it as a religious question, none other than that of God and immortality. "Socialism," he wrote, "is not only a problem of labour or of what is called the fourth class but is even more concerned with atheism, a modern incarnation of godlessness, the tower of Babel built without God, not to raise earth to heaven but to bring heaven down to earth." Socialism answers the everlasting question of a world-wide union of human beings, the organization of a kingdom of this world, and it is in Russian socialism that its religious nature is especially noticeable. Russian socialism is entirely apocalyptic, looking for a catastrophic issue to history. In Russia revolutionary socialism has never been regarded as a passing form of the economic and political organization of society but as a definitive and absolute condition, a solution of the destinies of mankind and the beginning of the establishment of God's kingdom on earth.

"What have Russian boys been doing so far, some of them at least?" says Ivan Karamazov. "Take this stinking pub, for example, where they meet and sit together in a corner. They've never met before, and when they go out of here they won't see each other again for the next forty years. But what do they talk about for the moment that they're here? Nothing but universal problems: Is there a God? Does the immortal soul exist? Those who don't believe in God discuss socialism and anarchism and the reorganization of mankind on a new pattern, which are the same questions, only tackled from the other way up." That shows the apocalyptic nature of those "Russian boys." It was at these discussions

in "stinking pubs" that Russian socialism and
Russian revolution first made their appearance, and
Dostoievsky saw exactly where these talks would
lead. "Shigalev watched as if he were waiting for
the destruction of the world, a destruction not
according to prophecies that cannot be fulfilled, but
definitely, on the morning of the day after to-
morrow, exactly at five and twenty minutes past
ten." All the "maximalist" Russian revolutionaries
have watched like Shigalev, with that apocalyptic or
nihilistic gaze which disowns historical ways, the
effort of culture and its gradual progress. Russian
socialism is leavened with nihilism, the arch-enemy
of cultural values and historical survivals, but it is
more easy to determine the nature of socialism in
general from this extreme form than from the more
moderate and refined forms current in Europe.

Socialism is a manifestation of the spirit. It claims
to be concerned with nothing short of final things, it
wants to be a new religion and to respond to man's
religious needs. As an eternal element, integral
socialism controlling the destiny of human society,
it cannot be associated with any particular material
and economic organization. It does not intend to
replace capitalism, for they are of the same flesh and
blood and cover the same ground. But it does mean
to replace Christianity, and to replace it by socialism,
for it is itself full of the messianic spirit and claims to
be the bearer of a gospel of mankind saved from its

misery and suffering.   Moreover, socialism has
sprouted in Jewish soil. It is the secular form of the
old Hebrew millenarianism, Israel's hope in a
miraculous earthly kingdom and temporal bliss. It
was not by chance that Karl Marx was a Jew. He
cherished the hope for the future appearance of a
messiah, the inverse of the Jesus whom the Hebrews
had rejected; but for him the elect of God, the
messianic people, was the proletariat and he
invested that class with all the attributes of the
chosen race. Dostoievsky did not have the most
perfect theoretical forms of socialism in front of him;
he did not know Marx and in fact knew socialism
only in its French form. But this did not prevent
his genius from foreseeing in it all its development
under Marx and the whole movement associated
therewith. Marxian socialism is constructed in such
a way that it appears antithetical to Christianity
from every point of view: there is between the two
doctrines precisely that resemblance that arises
from contrariness. Dostoievsky went further and
more deeply than the most understanding of the
marxists themselves in laying bare socialism's hidden
nature, and at the heart of its revolutionary godless
variety he discerned the very principle and spirit of
Antichrist. Not that he looked at it from the view-
point of bourgeois principles; on the contrary, he was
more radically opposed to the bourgeois spirit than
the socialists themselves, who are, fundamentally,

led captive by it. He was indeed a socialist himself in a manner of speaking: an "Orthodox Christian socialist," hostile to revolutionary socialism at every point, intent solely on the City of God and not on the building of any tower of Babel. Socialism can be fought successfully only on the spiritual plane, as Dostoievsky fought it, and not on the ground of the bourgeois interests against which it maintains its claims.

The inward principle of socialism is disbelief in God and in the immortality and freedom of the human spirit. Therefore does the socialist religion welcome the three temptations that our Lord refused in the wilderness—the temptations of stones turned to bread, of the kingdoms of the world, and of social miracle. It is not a religion for free sons of God but for slaves to necessity, children of the dust whose spiritual primacy has been snatched away from them. If life has no absolute meaning, if there be no eternity, then there is nothing left for men to do but to emulate Versilov's utopia, get together and organize world-happiness. Socialist religion is summed up by the Grand Inquisitor: "All the millions of human creatures will be happy. . . . We shall make them work, but in their spare time we shall organize their life like a children's game, with children's songs and cantatas and innocent dances. We shall allow them even sin, knowing they are so weak and helpless. . . . We shall give them an unexciting modest happiness

suitable to the feeble creatures that they are." This
religion says to Christianity: "Thou art proud of
thine elect, but thou hast only the elect while we
give comfort to all. . . . With us everybody will be
happy. . . . We shall persuade them that they will
only become free when they have given up their
freedom to us." The religion of the heavenly bread
is aristocratic, a religion for chosen ones, "the tens
of thousands of the great and strong"; the religion
for "the millions of others, numerous as grains of
sand on the shore, who are weak" is the religion of
earthly bread which has written on its banner,
"Feed men first, and then ask them to be good." And
man, beguiled by this socialist religion, has sold his
spiritual freedom for an illusion of material bread;
its representatives "put it forward as a virtue in
themselves that they have conquered freedom with
the sole object of making people happy." "Nothing
has ever or anywhere been more insupportable for
man and for society than freedom. But thou seest
these stones in this parched and torrid wilderness?
Turn them into bread and mankind will run after
thee like a flock of sheep, grateful and obedient but
fearful lest thou withdraw thy bounty." And finally
this religion says to Christ: "Thou didst refuse the
one infallible banner that was offered thee, beneath
which all men would have come unquestioningly to
bow before thee—the banner of earthly bread. Thou
didst reject it in the name of freedom and the bread

of Heaven. . . . I tell thee, man has no more urgent
anxiety than to find someone to whom he can hand
over this freedom with which the unfortunate creature is born.''

The first object of the socialist religion then is to
overturn that freedom of the human spirit which
introduces an irrational principle into life along with
numberless sufferings. Life ought to be submitted to
the collective judgment and reduced to one clear
operation that would leave no loose ends.   This
cannot be done without first putting an end to freedom, and to do that man must be deluded by the
transformation of stones into bread. Man is unhappy
and his history is tragic because he is endowed with
spiritual liberty: force him to renounce that, win
him over by an illusive offer of bread, and it will
then be possible to bring about happiness in the
world.   In *Letters from the Underworld* ''the gentleman with a cynical and sneering face'' appears as a
representative of the irrational element that disturbs
the organization of social harmony and welfare
because this sense of initial liberty is fermenting in
him, and it is dearer to him than his dinner. There
Dostoievsky made a very important discovery in
social philosophy. The sufferings of mankind, the
want by many individuals even of their daily bread,
are not due to the fact that man is exploited by man
or one class by another class (as socialism teaches),
but to the fact that man is born a free spiritual

creature; and such an one may prefer rather to go hungry than to lose his freedom of spirit and be enslaved to material bread. Human freedom involves liberty of choice, liberty of good and evil, and, in consequence, irrationality, suffering, and tragedy in life. Here, as always, Dostoievsky uncovers a hidden dialectic: Freedom of spirit means freedom for evil, and not for good only; but freedom for evil results in self-will, and self-will leads to insurrection against the source of spiritual freedom. So unchecked self-will ends by denying freedom and refusing it. Socialism embodies this destructive self-will and self-affirmation. Liberty is a burden, its path a way of the cross, and man in revolt seeks to throw it off. Thus freedom dies away into compulsion and slavery. Dostoievsky knew only one way out of this contradiction: Jesus Christ. In Christ freedom is given grace, wedded to infinite love, and no longer need become its own opposite, while the utopia of social happiness and perfection requires that it be reduced and limited. This can be seen in Shigalev's system, in Peter Verhovensky's, and in the doctrine of the Grand Inquisitor which, under a mask of Catholicism, really teaches the socialist religion of material bread and the social ant-heap.

Dostoievsky often refers to the bond that he thought he had detected between socialism and Catholicism, socialism being to him nothing but a secularized Catholicism. That is why the Legend of the Grand Inquisitor, to which I shall devote a separate chapter, was written against both the one and the other, though I am inclined to think that it was written more against socialism, Catholicism appearing only in an exterior form. The ideas of the Grand Inquisitor correspond surprisingly with those of Verhovensky, Shigalev, and his other representatives of revolutionary socialism, and this was because Dostoievsky had made up his mind that the papacy would finally ally itself with communism, on the ground that the papal idea and the socialist idea are one and the same conception of the compulsory organization of an earthly kingdom! In his eyes the two systems make a parallel denial of freedom of conscience and, having misunderstood the mediaeval doctrine of "the two swords," he claimed that the Roman Church aimed at temporal dominion and had grasped the sword of Caesar; thus she had pushed the peoples of Europe further along the road which must end in socialism. "France," he notes in the Diary, "even in the revolutionaries of the Convention, in her atheists, socialists, and now her communists, has always been and still is the country *par excellence* of Catholicism, infected by its letter and spirit. France, through the mouth of her most explicit atheists, proclaimed *Liberté, Egalité, Fraternité ou la mort* exactly as the Pope would do if he had to formulate and proclaim a Catholic liberty, equality, and fraternity; they are his words and it is his spirit, the authentic words and spirit of the popes of the Middle Ages. French socialism to-day is nothing but the direct and faithful sequel of the Catholic idea, its full and final expression, its inevitable conclusion elaborated through the ages. For French socialism is essentially the *compulsory* union of men, an idea inherited from ancient Rome which Catholicism has kept integrally." It must be admitted that Dostoievsky's knowledge of Catholicism was neither deep nor exact.

To him the French Revolution was a variant reincarnation of the old Roman formula of a universal union, and the same formula would govern the coming social upheaval; and if in the Franco-Prussian war he took sides with Protestant Germany it was in the hope that she would weaken this idea of an enforced fusion of men common to French Catholicism and socialism. In his time socialism was furthest developed in France: as I have said, he did not know the social-democracy that was arising in Germany and was quite ignorant of Marxism. Of course, it was a great mistake to identify Catholicism, so marvellously rich and varied, with the errors and excesses of the theocratic idea; the Catholic world has produced Francis of Assisi and many other great saints and mystics, it has the authentic Christian life and a religious mind of infinitely complex diversity. Nevertheless, Dostoievsky insisted on his analogy between the con-

trary Catholic and socialist principles. The socialist
state, he said, was not a secular but a confes-
sional state, like a country in which a church
is "established": strictly speaking, only those are
citizens in the fullest sense who profess the domi-
nant religion; the socialist state recognizes only one
"true faith," to which it tries to compel all men
without leaving any freedom of choice. But it was
just the same in the Orthodox Byzantine empire:
Eastern Orthodoxy was very far from having
avoided the deformation of Caesarism and the sup-
pression of spiritual liberty. Extremes meet, and on
occasion the freedom of the human spirit is as much
denied in Christian practice as by its opponent
socialism—and this is inevitable whenever temporal
are put before spiritual ends.

Dostoievsky examined and set forth the nature of
revolutionary socialism and its consequences in the
system of Shigalev, wherein is already found the
principle that was afterwards developed by the
Grand Inquisitor, though without his romantic sadness and personal impressiveness. There is something hopelessly commonplace about Shigalev's revolutionary ideas. Peter Verhovensky explains their
essentials to Stavroguin: "To level mountains is a
great idea, and not at all absurd. . . . There is no
need of education: we've had enough science. We
can go on collecting material for thousands of years

without its help—what we do need is organized obedience. . . . The thirst for culture is really an aristocratic thirst. The moment you have the family or love you get the desire for property. We will slay that desire: we will give a free hand to drunkenness and slander and private informers; we will allow the most unheard-of licentiousness; we'll stifle every genius in its cradle. Everything shall be reduced to a common denominator. Complete equality. . . . Only the necessary is necessary, that will be the motto of the whole world for the future. But there is a need for shocks and upheavals, and we, the directors, will see that they are provided. For slaves must be kept in hand. Absolute submission— no individuality whatsoever—but once in thirty years Shigalev will let them have a dust-up and they will all begin to eat each other: we can allow this, up to a point only, as a precaution against bo edom. Boredom is an aristocratic sensation. . . . Each belongs to all and all to each. All the slaves are equal in their slavery. . . . The first thing to do is to lower the level of education, science, and ability. A high standard of knowledge and capability is possible only for good intellects, and they are not wanted."

This enforced general levelling, this triumph for the transfer of the murderous law of entropy* into

* *Entropy*: "Measure of the unavailability of a system's thermal energy for conversion into mechanical work" (*Concise Oxford Dictionary*).

the social sphere, does not mean a victory for democracy. There will not be any democratic liberty, for
democracy never wins in revolutions. A tyrannical
minority will govern, on the basis of this deper-
sonalization and levelling-down. "Boundless liberty
leads me on to boundless tyranny," says Shigalev.
"But I may add that there is no solution to the
world-problem except my own." Here there can be
detected the fanaticism that springs from obsession
by a false idea, the obsession that leads to a radical
degradation of personality and ultimate loss of
humanity. Dostoievsky studied the process in the
disordered dreaming of the revolutionaries and
"youth" of Russia, even to the destruction of the
notion of being in all its richness. He believed that
social "castle-building," so far from being an
innocent amusement, was an endemic disease of the
Russian soul; he diagnosed it and forecast its course.

Those who in their wilfulness and rash self-sufficiency say that they love and sympathize with man
more than God does, who reject the divinely-
created world and boast that they can make a better
one in which there will be no evil and suffering, such
people are of necessity moving towards the kingdom
of Shigalev, for that is the only way God's work
can be corrected. As the *staretz* Zosima says: "Indeed,
they have more imaginative fancies than we. They
aim at organizing justly, but they have rejected
Christ and will end by flooding the earth with blood,

for blood cries for blood and he who takes the sword shall perish by it. Were it not for Christ's covenant, men would destroy one another down to the last pair." Prophetic words.

Dostoievsky showed that sentimentality and lack of honour were at the root of Russian revolutionary socialism: "Socialism is propagated among us chiefly by sentimentalism." But sentimentalism is a degraded emotion and a false sort of compassion that often ends in cruelty. Peter Verhovensky says to Stavroguin: "Our teaching is at bottom a negation of honour and by openly admitting dishonour we can easily attract any Russian." And Stavroguin replies, "The right to dishonour. For that they will all come to us, to the last man." Furthermore, Verhovensky asserts the importance to the revolution of such people as Fedka Katorjnik and similar blackguards: "They are a nice little lot, who could be very useful on occasions, though time would be lost in constantly keeping an eye on them." Continuing his analysis of revolutionary factors, Verhovensky says: "The most important element, the cement that binds everything together, is shame at having any opinion of one's own. That is indeed a strength, a continual influence towards the condition in which no one has any particular personal ideas in his head; he would be ashamed to." All the psychic factors of the revolution are evidence that, at its source and all through, it denies individual personality, its excellence, responsibility, and absolute value. Revolutionary morality does not recognize personality as the foundation of every moral estimate and judgment; it is wholly impersonal and denies all moral autonomy, admitting that it uses human persons as a means and material, that it allows the employment of any means that will forward the victory of the revolutionary thing. The revolution is by nature "amoral," placing itself above any consideration of good and evil (and in this respect the counter-revolution is exteriorly very like it). Dostoievsky opposed the revolution and its morality on behalf of the dignity of human personality and its moral value.

Revolution is madness, an obsession that attacks the personality, paralyses its freedom, and subjects it completely to an impersonal and unhuman force. Even its leaders do not know by what spirit they are possessed; they seem active, but in reality they are passive in the hands of the evil spirits they have let loose within themselves.   Joseph de Maistre emphasized the passive character of the leaders of the French Revolution in his book of *Considérations sur la France*. Man in revolt loses his autonomy: he comes under the power of an impersonal unhuman force. There lies the secret of revolution, the inhumanity from which arise dishonour, absence of private opinion, the tyranny of some and the subjection of others. Dostoievsky's conception of the world made him set the personal principle, the excellence and

absolute worth of personality, against the antichristian lie of impersonal collectivism, the false
universality of the socialist religion.

But "smerdyakovism" as well as "shigalevism"
has its day at a revolution. Ivan Karamazov and
Smerdyakov are two phenomena of Russian nihilism,
two forms of its mutiny, two aspects of the same
reality. Ivan is an evolving philosophical manifestation of the nihilist revolt: Smerdyakov is its mean
and subaltern expression; the one moves on the
plane of the intellect, the other in life's basement.
Smerdyakov translates the godless dialectic of his
half-brother into action and embodies his interior
punishment. (There are far more Smerdyakovs than
Ivans among mankind at large and the same holds
true for revolutions, which are movements of people
in mass.) Smerdyakov puts into practice the principle that "everything is allowable." Ivan kills his
father in spirit, Smerdyakov gives effect to the
thought and commits the crime in fact. In the same
way revolution inevitably becomes guilty of parricide, abolishing every filial tie and justifying the
violent separation of son from father by the fact that
the father was a weak and vicious man. This bloody
relation between son and father constitutes "smerdyakovism." When he has done the deed which Ivan
did in thought, Smerdyakov asks him: "You said
yourself that everything is allowable, so why are you
so frightened?" Just so the Smerdyakovs of the revo-

lution, when they have effectively actualized the proposition that everything is allowable, have the right to ask their Ivans, "And now, why are you so frightened?" The mutual relationship between Smerdyakov and Ivan is an excellent type of the relationship between "the people" and the *intelligentzia* at a time of revolution, and the Russian revolution has fulfilled and confirmed Dostoievsky's prophecy. The lackey Smerdyakov hated Ivan who had taught him atheism and nihilism, and, when he has uprisen and shown by his deeds that "everything is allowable," in his country's hour of mortal danger he says, "I hate Russia and everything about her." For with the revolutionary denial of personality there goes a complete break with our forefathers and the past, we are given a religion of killing in place of a religion of a rising from the dead. The assassination of Shatov is a concrete result of revolution.

There are three possible solutions to the problem of how may be brought about the harmony of the world, paradise, life in the heart of good: it may be attained, without suffering or creative effort, without universal tragedy, and without the freedom to refuse it; or it may be made the peak of earthly history, achieved at the price of the unnumbered sufferings and tears of all the generations that have served only as stepping-stones towards it; or mankind may reach it through freedom and accepted suffering on a plane

that every man who lives and suffers may attain at
will, that is, the kingdom of God. Dostoievsky reso-
lutely refused the first two solutions and accepted the
third.

There is a complexity in his dialectic that sometimes makes it difficult to understand exactly where
he stood himself. How much of the thoughts
expressed by the hero of the *Letters from the Underworld* or by Ivan Karamazov was his own? What was
his attitude to Versilov's earthly paradise or to the
one set out in the "Dream of a Funny Man"?* His
system of ideas is highly dynamic and contradictory:
it is no use stopping one in motion and asking for a
plain "yes" or "no" about it. He saw an effective
truth in the reaction of the man-from-the-under-
world or of Ivan Karamazov against the religion of
progress and its future world-harmony, so to that
extent he was on their side and rebelled with them.
His dialectic found fundamental contradictions in
the doctrine of progress. It may mean a future paradise and universal happiness for those who are there
to enjoy them, but it is death to endless generations
who have prepared the way by their labours and
sufferings. Can a religious and moral conscience
accept harmony bought at such a price, can it co-
operate with progress on this condition? Dostoievsky's own voice can be heard in the words of Ivan
Karamazov: "Quite definitely, I don't accept this

* In the *Diary of a Writer*, under April 1877.

divine world and although I know it exists I refuse
to recognize it. It's not that I don't accept God;
it's the world created by him that I don't and can't
accept. Let me explain: I am as convinced as a
child that suffering will be healed and disappear,
that all the shocking ludicrousness of human contradiction will vanish like a pitiable mirage, like the
product of low and feeble people, a fragment of the
euclidian mind that it is; and that at the end of the
world, at the moment of everlasting harmony, something so glorious will come to pass that it will ravish
every heart, soothe all anger, atone for man's every
crime and all the blood that he has spilled, and all
this so thoroughly that what man has undergone will
be not only pardonable but justified. All that will
happen—but in spite of it I do not and I will not
accept it. . . . I have not suffered in order that my
sorrows and sins may enrich some harmony that is to
be. . . . I ask you, if all must suffer to pay for eternal
harmony, what have children got to do with it? It
is absolutely beyond understanding that they should
suffer and pay for it. Why should they too be used
as manure? . . . I renounce the higher harmony
altogether. It is not worth the tears of a single tortured child beating its breast with its little fist and
crying out with guiltless sobs to 'good, kind God'
from the floor of its noisome hovel. It's not worth it,
because those tears are not atoned for, and unless
they are you can't have any harmony."

Thus does Ivan Karamazov reject any distinction between good and evil and refuse any part in the building of human destiny, because it costs too much. He returns to God his ticket of admission to his universal harmony. Does Dostoievsky without qualification share the arguments of Ivan Karamazov? Both yes and no. Ivan's dialectic is that of the "euclidian mind," of an atheist who will not recognize any mind above life. But in his revolt he lets slip a truth that is Dostoievsky's own. If there be no God, if there be no redeemer and no atonement, if there be no meaning in the process of history, then we ought to repudiate the world and its coming harmony and to regard the idea of progress as a thing detestable. Ivan surpasses the usual prophets of the religion of progress and revolutionary socialism in that he rejects the world as well as God. A masterpiece of foresight. Ordinarily an exaltation of the world is joined to the notion of atheism: naturally, if nothing exists except this world. The higher mind that is denied to life is transferred to the future harmony. But Dostoievsky shows the logical end of the revolt against God and a divine meaning in things: the atheism of the "euclidian mind" *must* also reject the world, rise against the future harmony, repudiate the latest religion, "Progress." He says that this last stage coincides with a positive truth: when we have been led to not-being, denial of the world, and a realization of the hollow mockery of the reli-

gion of progress, then there is only one way left—
and it leads to Jesus Christ. That is why Dostoievsky
may be said to be half with Ivan Karamazov. If
there is a divine meaning (that the "euclidian mind"
cannot see), if there is a redeemer, if earthly life is
itself an atonement, if the definitive harmony of the
world is in the kingdom of God and not in a worldly
kingdom, then this world can be accepted and its
history with all its numberless sufferings can be justified.

The growth of self-will and revolt is therefore
suicidal in that they have eventually to repudiate
what they formerly upheld. From a refusal of the
legacy of history there follows a refusal of its latest
results and final goals, of the religion of progress and
of socialism. It is not possible to justify and receive
what ought to be without justifying and receiving
what has been: past and future are in one single
destiny; "fragmentary time" must be vanquished
and past, present, and future made one in eternity.
Only then can the history of the world—and the
tears of the children—be justified: if there is immortality the historical process can be accepted; but if
there is none, it has to be rejected. Therefore Dostoievsky rejected the second of the solutions set out
above, which makes progress the sole condition of a
universal harmony; nor could he accept a harmony
based on the loss of freedom, a non-distinction
between good and evil, a harmony which the

tragedy of the world had never disturbed. There can be no return to a lost paradise. Man must attain harmony by freedom of choice and a free victory over evil; a compulsory harmony is worthless and does not correspond to the dignity of a divine race of beings (*cf.* the description of paradise in the "Dream of a Funny Man"). Man must tread the painful road of freedom to the end and, since the worship of mankind and of the world lead only to destruction and not-being, that end is the God-man, Jesus Christ, in whom alone are human liberty and divine harmony reconciled.

Dostoievsky, then, would solve the world's problem in the third way, and through the Church. He had his own theocratic utopia, which he opposed to the Catholic theocracy as well as to the socialist utopia of a temporal paradise: the Church is called to reign over the world. "The Church is not to be transformed into the State," says Father Paisy in *The Brothers Karamazov*: "That is Rome and her dream, and it is the third temptation of the Devil. On the contrary, it is the State that must be transformed into the Church, rise to her level, and become a church over the whole world. That idea is diametrically opposed to ultramontanism and to Rome, and it is the glorious mission of Orthodoxy to bring it about. Light must come from the East." In his view the Church is not yet the kingdom of God as Catholicism teaches, following St. Augustine; a kingdom

must arise in the Church, as it were by a new revelation, and for this actualization of the prophetical
gift of Christianity Dostoievsky looked. Moreover, it
was among the Russians, as an apocalyptic people,
that this religious happening should take place, they
should once and for all manifest the falsehood of
godless socialism and its revolution. Dostoievsky
met social hatred with social love, and the new era
of Christianity was to be marked by freedom and
brotherhood in Christ.

Like all the other Russian philosophers of religion
Dostoievsky was hostile to "bourgeois civilization,"
and he was opposed to western Europe in the same
measure that that civilization was in the ascendant
there. And he was in full conflict with the atheistic
anarchism and socialism, but there were nevertheless
oddly anarchistic and socialistic elements of a
Christian kind in his own theocratic visions; he never
properly worked out his notion of the State, and his
monarchism was distinctly anarchic. These considerations bring us to the religious messianism
which had so strong an influence on his social
theories.

CHAPTER VII

RUSSIA

DOSTOIEVSKY was essentially a Russian and a writer
about Russia, and the riddle of the Russian soul can
be read in him: he was an embodiment of it and all
its contradictions; men of the West see Russia in his
person. But he did more than reflect and portray
that soul in activity; he was the herald of the
"Russian idea" and of the consciousness of his
nation, with all its antinomies and restless uneasi-
ness, its humility and arrogance, its universal compassion and its national exclusivism. When, in his
famous speech on Pushkin,* he said to his countrymen, "Humble thyself, proud man!" the humbleness
that he commended was not simply humility. He
looked on the Russian people as the humblest on
earth, but he was proud of this humility. And that,
indeed, seems to be the pride of the Russians. Dostoievsky saw his people as the "God-bearers,"
unique among their kind, and consciousness of this
particularist messianism is not compatible with
humility; the feeling and mentality of the Jews of old
were reborn in them.

* At the unveiling of a monument to Pushkin at Moscow in June
1880, six months before his death. TR.

His attitude towards Europe was equally contradictory. We shall see that he was a real European patriot, who reverenced her past and her holy things and said in her praise what no European has said. This attitude illustrates the universalism of Russia, her ability to live to herself and yet to make her own all that is fine in the world. On the other hand, Dostoievsky denied that the people of Europe were Christian, and drew up a sentence of death against her. He was deeply chauvinistic and there was a deal of injustice in his judgments of other peoples, the French and Poles, for instance, and in general the Jews. The Russians' consciousness of themselves has always made them either rail violently against everything Russian and divorce themselves from their native land or else affirm her equally violently and with an exclusivism that makes other peoples seem to belong to a lesser breed. Our national feeling has never been well-balanced, quietly sure of itself, free from hysteria. So it was with Dostoievsky: his national consciousness never reached the serenity of spiritual manhood, it was always ill with the Russian complaint.

It must be understood that the structure of the Russian soul is all its own and completely different from that of Westerners. The more penetrating minds of the West realize this well enough, and are attracted by the puzzle it presents. The Russian East is a huge world, as big as western Europe and all its

L—d

peoples put together. It is a plain of vast extent, with no strongly-marked outline or landmarks; there is neither the confused mass of mountains and valleys nor anything defining the particular shape of any region. And the life of Russia flows along the infinitude of her plains. The geography of the land coincides with the geography of her soul, a symbolic expression of its spirit. The evenness, the unending distances, the indefiniteness of the features of the Russian earth embody the nature of the Russian man and typify similar qualities in his soul. It is not a matter of chance that such-and-such a people lives in such-and-such a land, amid such-and-such natural surroundings: there is an inward bond between them; the nature of a countryside is determined by the people who live in it. Everywhere on the face of the earth can be felt the difficulty man has had to conquer it, to give it form, to bring it under cultivation. In Russia man is dominated by the land and its elements, and indiscipline is common to both. The soul is drawn to infinite flat distances and is lost in them; it cannot bear to live within the clearly marked frontiers of a differentiated culture and submit to an order which it does not find in its physical surroundings. The soul of the European is a castle fortified by a religious and cultural discipline; that of the Russian is apocalyptic and fluid by "build" and inclination, ever gliding towards the beckoning horizon, especially to that far one which seems to hide the end of the world. It is easily carried away, uprooted, always inclined to go wandering about its native *steppes*, and its formlessness and indiscipline have meant the lack of any real conserving instinct among Russians: they wear themselves out for nothing at all and, as it were, disappear into space, as the poet Biely says.

There is but little for which Russia has any reverence or attachment. The Russian faces a cultural crisis unconcernedly and has not yet succeeded in making a culture really his own. That is where his characteristic nihilism comes in: he will light-heartedly renounce science and art, nation and home, and all other ties, in his hankering after a far-away, unknowable kingdom. The far-reaching spiritual experiences that Dostoievsky narrates are possible only to the Russian soul; the formative cultures, traditions, and rational fixity of Europe would have been a grave obstacle to such researches, and that is why it is not conceivable that such a thinker should emerge anywhere but in Russia.

Dostoievsky was in his way a "populist" (*narodnik*), believing in a religious "populism." This particular sort of love for the people is a phenomenon unknown in the West, for it is only in Russia that we meet the everlasting opposition of the "*intelligentzia*" and "the people," with its idealization of "the masses" that goes to the length of bowing down before them and

looking for God and truth among them. Populism
was always a sign of the weakness of the cultural
movement and the lack of a healthy consciousness of
its mission. When Russia was an immense kingdom
of peasants with the Tzar at their head it included a
very limited number of classes, with a relatively
weak and small cultured *élite* and a conservative
machinery of government that was hopelessly swollen
and unwieldy. In such a social structure the intellectual class felt helpless in face of the dark ocean of
the people at large and in danger of being drowned
in it. The imperial power, which enjoyed a religious
sanction in popular consciousness, both safeguarded
the educated class and persecuted it. The state of
mind of this class (which at a certain moment gave
itself the name of "the *intelligentzia*") was tragic
during the nineteenth century, completely patho-
logical. There were no strong cultural traditions in
Russian history and there were no organic ties with
any differentiated society of classes proud and well-
established in a glorious past, and this cultured
minority found itself caught between the tzarist
authority and the life of the people: it was in a cleft
stick. So, by an instinct of spiritual self-preservation,
it began to idealize one or the other of these elements
by turn, or even both together, in an endeavour to
find a *point d'appui*. Eventually it admitted a number
of the common people to its ranks (it was then that it
took the name *intelligentzia*) and surrendered to of

the element that threatened to swallow it. Henceforward "the people" represents for the *intelligentzia* a mysterious and compelling force which holds the secret of life and is the depository of some special truth; in the people the intellectuals found the God they had lost.

The *intelligentzia* did not feel itself an organic part of Russian life, for its roots and its unity were gone; its integrity had been handed over to the people, through whom alone it now lived and knew truth. This intellectual class did not have the courage to preach its message to the people and fulfil its duty of bringing light into their dark places; it was doubtful of its office of enlightener, it did not believe in itself, it questioned the intrinsic worth of culture. This is a bad state of mind for the discharge of culture's undeniable mission. The intellectuals came to cast suspicion on it from moral, religious, and social points-of-view alike: culture was a fruit of injustice, bought at too high a price, it signified a rupture with the people's life, a violation of its organic integrity: it was a crime against the people, a going-out from among them, a forgetfulness of them. This feeling of its guilt pursued the Russian *intelligentzia* throughout the nineteenth century and undermined its creative energy; and it was due, I must emphasize it, to the fact that the educated class was not sufficiently conscious of the absolute value of culture and even allowed a moral doubt about it.

This is very characteristic of Russian populism: truth is not to be looked for in culture and its objective aims but in "the people," a stream of organic life, wherein, too (and not in culture and the spirit), resides religious life. I am speaking here of the first principles of populism, independent of various tendencies and shades of opinion. Actually, there were two main tendencies, naturalistic and religious, and both forms were expressive of the same psychology. The extreme "right" and the extreme "left," slavophil populists and atheistic socialist populists, have notable points of resemblance: there is the same idealization of the people and reactionary hostility to culture, there is a similar inhibition of the personal principle and of the cultivation of personality, responsibility, and honour, a similar incapacity for spiritual autonomy, a similar intolerance, a similar seeking for truth outside rather than within oneself; the disease of the national soul is manifest at either pole. The absence of an age of chivalry in Russia has been disastrous for her moral culture. Her collectivism has shown more than once how insufficiently awakened the personal spirit is, the personality of men remaining absorbed in the natural current of the people's existence—and therefore that is where the populist theory looks for God and truth.

What exactly is "the people" for this theory? The answer even to that question is extremely uncertain and difficult. For most populists the people is not the nation,understanding by that term a whole organism, including all social classes and states, all historical generations, the "intellectual" and the nobleman as well as the peasant, the shopkeeper and the artisan as well as the labourer. The word "people" has not for them its ontological and defined meaning but carries a social and class signification, indicating principally peasants and "workers," the lower classes of society who live by their physical labour. The nobility, manufacturers and traders, scholars, men-of-letters, artists, are not an organic part of the people; they are, indeed, set up against them as the *bourgeoisie* or *intelligentzia*. It is, of course, this class conception that rules in revolutionary and materialist populism, but the curious thing is that it also predominated in religious populism and in Slavophilism, even though it was in flagrant contradiction with the principles of the slavophil conscience. For the slavophils—as for Dostoievsky—the people was above all the simple folk, particularly the peasants, from whose unity and truth the intellectual class was separated in their eyes. The *muzhik* was the guardian of the true faith. If I was a noble or a business-man, a scholar or a writer, an engineer or a physician, I could not feel myself as part of "the people"; I had to regard them as a mysterious energy opposed to myself, to which I must kneel as to a bearer of a higher truth. There was no possibility of an immanent relation for me with them; it could be only transcendent, for the people above all was the "not-I," opposed to myself, in whose presence I felt a sense of guilt. That is a purely slavish idea, excluding all freedom of spirit and consciousness of a personal spiritual liberty. This illusory populism was Dostoievsky's own, and it was in striking contrast with the words on the subject of the Russian nobility that he put into the mouth of Versilov: "I cannot but respect our nobility. During the course of centuries it has created a certain type of high culture like no other in the world, a culture which takes upon itself the sufferings of all. It is a Russian type and as it is rooted in the higher and more cultivated class of our people I am able to have the honour to partake of it. This group is guardian of the Russia of the future. It may number a thousand (perhaps more, perhaps less), but all Russia has existed solely to produce that thousand."

The greatest of Russian geniuses, even at the height of their spiritual life and creative powers, were unable to bear the lofty peaks and haughty freedom of the spirit; they were afraid of solitude and hurled themselves down into the flat places of the life of the people, hoping by so doing to reach a higher truth. They had not the lyricism which belongs to the mountain-tops; they dreaded the loneliness, the forsakenness, the cold, and sought refuge in the lukewarm stream of the people's collective existence. Herein the Russian genius (*e.g.*, Dostoievsky) differs

absolutely from the European genius (*e.g.*, Nietzsche),
and the first to experience Russian consciousness, the
slavophils, shared this national characteristic. They
certainly held a very high position in European
culture and were the most cultured of all Russians;
they understood that culture cannot be only national
and in that respect were nearer to the Western mind
than the "westernizing" Russians themselves. But
they surrendered to the peasants, not having the
strength to defend their truth as a national truth
common to everybody; and they also looked upon
the people, "the folk," as in opposition to the cultured class—a mistake which had dire consequences
for the national consciousness. The irreligious "left"
garnered the harvest of this identification of the
people with a class. The gulf between *intelligentzia*
and "people" was widened, a *national* consciousness
became impossible, and only the notion of *populism*
remained. All the time there were in the heart o
Slavophilism seeds of a larger and more living understanding of the people, as a nation, as a mystical
body; but the slavophils fell victims to the malady
of the intellectuals, and so did Dostoievsky himself.

Dostoievsky's populism is of a kind peculiar to him,
in that it is religious. The slavophils, to be sure,
believed the Russian people to be the best, nay, the
only Christian people in the world, and Koshelev
used to say that without their Orthodoxy they would

"be nothing but muck." But Dostoievsky's religious faith in his people was quite different. The slavophils felt themselves to be solidly established upon their landed property and suspected no impending catastrophe. Dostoievsky, on the contrary, belonged to the new era that was sensible of change and looked for its religion in the Book of the Apocalypse. His conception of the people embraced their messianic relation to the whole world: the slavophils were still provincials compared with him. His attitude towards Europe was infinitely more intricate and delicate, and they were not in agreement about the history of their country. For example, Dostoievsky did not feel called upon to idealize the Russia of before Peter the Great, but gave an enormous importance to his period and to the rise of Petersburg. What interested him was man's destiny in after-Peter Russia, the tragic and complicated ordeal of the men who were uprooted at that time. In this he followed Pushkin, whose vision and writing of the spectral element in Petersburg fascinated him while the traditional and countrified manners of Moscow were quite foreign to him. Therefore Dostoievsky was not a slavophil in the accepted sense of the word, any more than Constantine Leontiev was; they were men of a new pattern, looking towards the coming calamity, animated by a dynamism of which the slavophils had none.

There is a whole series of hostile allusions to the
slavophils in the Diary, and many of them are unjust
as well. They "have a rare capacity for misunderstanding their [own people] and for understanding
nothing of the realities of their own times." He
defends the "westernizers" against them: "Is it a
fact that the westernizers had less instinct for the
Russian spirit than the slavophils? . . . Seeing that
Occidentalism was at least more realist than Slavophilism, and that in spite of all its mistakes it was
more far-reaching, it has continued on the side of
movement while the slavophils have everlastingly
stayed where they were and even claimed much
honour for so doing. Occidentalism has had the
audacity to put fundamental questions and pain-
fully to find the answers in its own consciousness, it
has known how to go back to the soil again to achieve
union with the people's elements and to find salvation in the earth. We for our part put forward as a
fact which we believe to be unalterable that the
influence of the slavophils towards the present conscious or unconscious return to the land (which is by
no means general) has been the lesser, very slight,
perhaps none at all." Dostoievsky valued the westernizers for their research and investigation, for the
wideness of their outlook, and for the energy of their
wills, while the slavophils troubled him because, as
an aristocracy, they stood apart from the difficulties
of life and from the literary movement, looking down

on everything from above. For him, the "Russian
boy," the atheists, the socialists, and the anarchists
were so many manifestations of the Russian mind,
and so was the "westernized" literature. To slavophil idealism he opposed the tragic reality of life.
He appreciated the nature and future results of the
inward tendencies that were gaining force and maintained the need for spiritual experiment; but his contemporary slavophils, those of the second generation,
were blind to all movements and afraid of experiments. Nor was their attachment to their native soil
of the same kind. Dostoievsky looked deep into the
Russian earth, down to the lowest strata whose
existence manifested itself only through earthquakes
and landslides; his rootedness was not fixed but
ontological, an understanding of the people's
mind and spirit in their very essence.

Dostoievsky put many of his own thoughts into the
mouth of Versilov, and Versilov's sympathetic view
of Europe is characteristic of Dostoievsky's own
attitude. The Russian is universal and the freest man
in the world; the Europeans "are not free as we are.
I alone, with my Russian melancholy, was then free.
. . . Every Frenchman is able to serve not only
France but mankind, but on the one condition that
he remains a Frenchman; it is the same with the
English and the Germans. In our times it is only
the Russian who has the faculty of being more and

more Russian as he becomes more European. That is the most radical difference between us and all others, and nobody is like us in this respect. In France, I am French; with a German, German; with a Greek of the past I should be a Greek—and none the less I remain an authentic Russian and serve Russia all the better, because I embody her essential idea.... Europe is as precious to a Russian as Russia: her every stone is lovely and valuable. Europe has been our home as much as Russia—nay, more! No one can love Russia more than I do, but I can never reproach myself because Venice and Rome and Paris with all their art and learning and history are yet more delectable to me. How dear they are to a Russian!—those old foreign stones, those miracles of God's ancient world, those ruins of holy marvels: they are more dear to us than even to them. . . . It is only Russia that lives for an idea and not for herself; and the remarkable thing is that for nearly a century she has lived not for herself but only for Europe." No slavophil could have subscribed to those words.

Ivan Karamazov speaks to the same effect: "I want to travel in Europe. I know that I shall find only a graveyard there, but it is the most beloved of graveyards. There sleep the dear dead, and the stones that cover them speak of such burning life in the past, of so passionate a faith in its work and its truth and its struggles and its learning, that I know beforehand I

shall fall on my knees and kiss those stones and weep
over them—and all the time be convinced in my
heart that it has long been a graveyard and nothing
else." Again, in the Diary: "What an awesome and
sacred thing Europe is! Gentlemen, according to you
we slavophil dreamers hate Europe. You don't
know how dear to us this Europe, the country of
holy marvels, really is. Do you know how dear to
us those marvels are? Do you know how we love and
reverence, more than fraternally, the great races
that live in Europe and all their grand, noble, and
exalted achievements? Do you know how our hearts
are wrung, how many tears we shed over the destiny
of those near lands, how we fear the dark clouds that
are massing on their horizon? No, gentlemen; you
europeanizers and westernizers will never love
Europe as do we, the dreaming slavophils whom you
represent as her traditional enemies." Neither westernizers nor slavophils properly so-called spoke
thus. Only Constantine Leontiev—and he was
neither one nor the other—wrote of the past of
Europe in like terms. Russian religious thinkers of
his type and Dostoievsky's, far from denying the
high culture of western Europe, estimated it at a
greater worth than did contemporary Europeans;
what they did deny was her new mercantile civilization with its middle-class spirit, and that they denounced as a betrayal of Europe's high tradition and
legacy of culture.

For many Russian thinkers the opposition between Russia and Europe was a conflict of two minds, two types of culture; it was an aspect of the war against the tendencies of an actual civilization which was destructive of spirit. Eastern slavophilism was a special aberration of this consciousness. There were two spirits fighting in the world, and the spirit of commercial civilization was beginning to win because the Christian principle of culture had been betrayed: material well-being was hiding heaven. That was the tendency of civilization throughout the world, but it was most clearly marked among European peoples. The Russians had been saved from it by their backwardness. But it was a mistake to deduce from this backwardness that a contemporary world-tendency had no effect on Russia and that her people were protected from it by the nature of their spirit. The religious inclinations in Russian thought and writing took on the hue of slavophilism and of the East as a protective colouring. Germany experienced a similar crystallization and consciousness of herself during the period of the great activity of Idealism and Romanticism there at the beginning of the nineteenth century; the idealist spirit, the romantic leanings, the predominance of high spiritual interests proclaimed themselves to be specifically German manifestations as opposed to the non-spiritual tendencies of France and England: the idea of German messianism dates from that time. But all this did not prevent Germany from failing in her spiritual mission and choosing the road of materialism.

The struggle between religious culture and irreligious civilization was always imminent in western Europe itself and was fought out there. The romantics, symbolists, and Catholics in nineteenth-century France, *e.g.*, Barbey d'Aurevilly, Villiers de l'Isle-Adam, Huysmans, Léon Bloy, were no less wounded by the spectacle of contemporary European civilization than were Dostoievsky and Leontiev, and they fought it with all their might; they, too, looked back to the Middle Ages as to their spiritual home. Again, Nietzsche, with his impassioned dream of a dionysiac culture, was a loud protest, in morbid terms, against the same triumphant advance of middle-class civilization. It is a universal theme and it cannot be regarded simply as an opposition between Russia and Europe, the East and the West. It is the contrast of two types of mind and culture, and both types were represented in Russia as in Europe; only it so happened that certain Russians felt it more keenly than anybody else. Even Herzen was more conscious of it than the Europeans of the 'forties. But it did not follow from this that the new irreligious civilization would not triumph in Russia and the spirit not be eclipsed. The marxists have arisen and thriven there. The struggle is now to save spirit, culture, and true civilization from extinction, and it is possible that in Russia they cannot survive.

Spirit and culture must not merely be brought nearer to one another, they must be identified, for, while civilization may lack spirituality altogether, culture is always spiritual: it is bound by its nature to a sacred tradition, to piety for the men and things of of times past. Dostoievsky discerned the division brought about in the movement of his day by the appearance of the spirit of Antichrist therein better than did anyone else, especially where Russia was concerned. Leontiev longed hopelessly till the end of his life to see the birth and growth of a new type of culture, reminiscent of that of the great past, which would stand up to the withered civilization of Europe; he sank into despair, for he saw instead the victorious progress in his country of that general levelling which he hated so much: it seemed to him in his anguish that "Russia had only one religious mission, and that was to give birth to Antichrist." The development of the idea of religious populism dealt grievous blows to Russia and at length itself fell into dissolution. Russian messianism has had a terrible destiny.

"If it is to remain a living force for any length of time every great people must believe that the salvation of the world resides in it and in it alone, that it exists to be at the head of all peoples, to gather them

M—d

round itself, and to lead them in a united body
towards a final end which it will have assigned to
them." In these words in the Diary Dostoievsky
stated the need for a messianic national consciousness. Such a notion does not involve any nationalistic exclusivism, at any rate at first. It is general-
ized and universal, a call to effect the salvation of
all peoples throughout the world, a task proposed by
Dostoievsky to the Russians as the God-bearers of
mankind. He was looking higher than nationalism.
The slavophils, on the other hand, who were
eminently nationalistic by definition and convinced
that the Russian people was a superior type of Christian culture, did not claim it as their duty to save
the world and discover universal truth. Dostoievsky
found the universalism of the Russian spirit in
Pushkin; he was struck by his "power of universal
sympathy, and his very complete, almost perfect,
assimilation of the genius of foreign peoples. . . .
This faculty is essentially Russian and Pushkin
truly shares it with all our people." He said, con-
trarily to the slavophils, that "our reaching-out
towards Europe, with all its enthusiasm and exag-
geration, has not been solely official and reasoned
but has been popular as well; it has fully coincided
with the desires of the common mind, and its final
object has certainly been a most exalted one. . . .
The Russian soul, the genius of the Russian
people, is probably better fitted than any other

to shelter the idea of world-wide unity and brotherhood."

Dostoievsky showed that the nomadism of the
Russians, their restless and rebellious wandering,
was a profoundly national trait: "In Aleko, Pushkin
has investigated and marvellously portrayed the
unhappy wanderer in his native land, the historical
Russian martyr." The furthest rovings of this wanderer were Dostoievsky's own study. "Only universal happiness can give peace to the Russian wanderer:
he will find rest in nothing less"—there in the home-
less vagabond is the universalist spirit of a whole
people. But here Dostoievsky's dynamism, rejecting
everything fixed and stable, involved him in a contradiction. The Russian wanderer has severed himself from his native soil: therein lie his transgression
and the reason of his creative sterility. But the
déraciné, whom he considered as a product of the
upper class, Dostoievsky looked upon with disdain, as
a "Russian nobleman and a citizen of the world";
he was for all that also a manifestation of the
national spirit. Such a contradictory judgment
would not be made by the slavophils, whose thought
had more unity.

But in general Dostoievsky loved this wanderer and
déraciné and was hugely interested in his destiny. He
regarded the *intelligentzia*, cut off from the people, as
highly characteristic, thereby showing that his religious populism was a juxtaposition of contradictory

notions. The fact is that when he preached "submission before the people" and the "search for truth
among the people" or "for the people's truth" he
meant by the word "people" a mystical organism,
the soul of the nation conceived as an immense and
mysterious whole of which the overwhelming
majority was made up of simple folk, *muzhiks*. Here
a finger can be laid on the inveterate mistake of this
populist notion. There is, in fact, no need to go
among the people to be in touch with them. The
wandering Russian, alone and cut off from his
origins, can still find his people and their life in the
depths of his own being, and belong to them from
the bare fact of his having this depth. The "popular"
element is not outside of myself, in the *muzhik*, but
within myself, in that inmost part of my being where
I am not like a closed monad. The single actual
relation that I have with those who constitute "the
people" is only on the surface; to become myself "of
the people" I don't require to be among peasants
and simple folk, for I have only to look inward to
my own spirit.

Dostoievsky was more "people" than the people
themselves, more than the whole peasant class put
together, and he did not find the "truth of the people" among the *muzhiks* (from whom he was empiric-
ally apart), for it was there, as I have said, in the
depth of his own spirit. And what was that truth?
"The Russian is unquestionably made to be pan-

european and world-embracing. To be a true and complete Russian means to be everybody's brother, a universal man—perhaps it means nothing else. All this Slavophilism and Occidentalism of ours is a huge mistake, though an historically necessary one. Europe, as a fief of the great aryan family, is as dear to an authentic Russian as Russia herself; it is a dependency of the native land, for we see the whole world as our heritage." In this conception of the Russians' predestined rôle Dostoievsky comes much nearer to Vladimir Soloviev than to the slavophils and the nationalists who followed them, but it involves the contradictions and dangers that beset all messianic statements.

The idea of messianism was first given to the world by the Hebrews of old, the chosen people of God among whom the Messiah was to be born, and there is no other messianism but the Hebraic. It was justified by the coming in due course of Jesus Christ, and after his earthly life all messianism was henceforward impossible among Christian peoples who, united in Christendom, became the elect of God. They have their mission, the call to spread the faith, but missionary consciousness is not the same thing as a messianic consciousness. Jewish messianism was based on a union and identification of religious and national elements, but messianic consciousness is not nationalistic (nationalism is always particularist),

it is universal. The Jews were not one people among
other peoples: they were the one and only people of
God, divinely chosen to save the world and prepare
his kingdom on earth; and messianism within
Christendom is always a rejudaization of Christianity, a return to the old identification of the
universal religion with a universal nation.   There
were indisputable elements of this transferred
Judaism in the claim that Russia was the "third
Rome," and this same Judaism manifested itself in a
still more striking way in the messianism of Poland.

Starting from the "third Rome" idea, Russian
messianic consciousness flourished throughout the
nineteenth century, and in the twentieth it reached
the culmination of its tragic destiny. The Russia of
the tzars was not much like a third Rome. Its church,
as Dostoievsky says, was paralytic, in a state of humiliating subjection to Caesar, and as they did not yet
possess their City of God Russian messianists had to
look forward to a future City: they hoped for the
coming of a new kingdom in Russia, the millennium
of Jesus Christ. Then imperial Russia collapsed, the
revolution severed the heavy chain that had bound
Church to State, and the country experienced the
actualization of a new kingdom of this world: but
instead of the "third Rome" it was the Third International. And the consciousness of those who made
the Third International was seen to be, in its own
way, messianic; they saw themselves as light-bearers

from the East, sent to enlighten the peoples of the West still plunged in the darkness of "the *bourgeoisie*." That is what Russian messianism led to; it is no longer to be found set out in the writings of the monk Philothey but in those of Bakunin and Lenin. And we have there a proof that at the root of this messianic consciousness there is an untruth, a false relationship between the religious element and the national element. Worship of the people is a sin, a sin fundamental to messianic consciousness, and it brings its own inevitable punishment.

The antinomies, temptations, and iniquities of the Russian messianic idea are summed up in the person of Shatov, in *The Possessed*. Of course, Dostoievsky himself was not Shatov, but he was fond of him and, as with all his other chief characters, there are elements of Dostoievsky in him. He says to Stavroguin: "Do you know which is at the present moment the only God-bearing people in the whole world, getting ready to renew and save the world in the name of the new god, the people to which the keys of life and of the new gospel are given? . . . . Up till now each people was only a people; it is time for every one to have its own particular god and rigorously to exclude all other gods whatsoever." That is a resurgence of pagan particularism, but later on Shatov comes back to the universalist pretensions of Judaism: "If a great people does not believe that the truth is to be found exclusively in itself, if it does not believe that it alone is able to revivify and save all the rest, that it is designed for that very purpose, then it is no longer a great people but only an ethnographical unit. . . . But there is only one truth and therefore only one people can have the truth of God, even though other nations may have great gods of their own. That one God-bearing people is the people of Russia." Then Stavroguin asks the crucial question—"Do you yourself believe in God or not?" And Shatov stammers excitedly: "I believe in Russia, I believe in her Orthodoxy. . . . I believe in the body of Christ. . . . I believe that a second coming will take place in Russia. . . ." "But in God, in God?" Stavroguin insists. "I . . . I will believe in God."

In this astounding conversation Dostoievsky throws into relief the falsehood of religious populism, the people-worship that waits on messianism. Many Russians used to, and still do, believe in the people more than in God, and want to go to him through them: people-worship is an essentially Russian fallacy. And the religious and "people's" elements are so mixed up in Russian consciousness that it is difficult to distinguish them, and in their formal religion they are often almost identified. The people believe in a "Russian Christ," who is the national god, a peasant god with their own characteristics—it is a pagan tendency in the very bosom of Orthodoxy. This narrow and exclusive religious nationalism, foreign to Western Christianity and purely negative in its attitude towards Catholicism, is completely out of accord with the universalist spirit of Christ. That Russian religion should have individual and particular characteristics is in no wise at variance with the universal character of Christianity, whose total unity is not an abstract but a concrete unity; but in Russian Christianity as it is there is grave danger of a predominance of the "people" element over the Universal Logos, of the soul over the spirit, a weakening of the masculine element. The danger can be seen in Dostoievsky himself: his deity is often the Russian god and not the universal God, and his intolerance is the Judaic trait in his religiousness.

Both revolutionary and reactionary tendencies are joined in Shatov, and he illustrates the kinship between them. The "maximalist" revolutionary and the "Black-hundreder" sometimes hardly differ from one another, and the points of resemblance are always striking. Both are deluded by people-worship: it upsets their reason and paralyses their personality; they are alike obsessed. Dostoievsky put this very clearly, for he felt both tendencies in himself. He perceived among his countrymen tides of affliction, of emotion, and of licentiousness that "populist" writers did not see. The *Khlisty* were a very characteristic manifestation, combining in effect Orthodoxy with the ancient native paganism.

Russian religiousness when it becomes ecstatic nearly always takes this or a similar form: the popular natural element proves stronger than the world-wide light of the Logos.

A break in the necessary relationship between the masculine and feminine elements, between spirit and soul, is the source of all the disorders of the Russian religious and national consciousness. The sea of suffering in which the people live is described with powerful intuition by Andrew Biely in his novel called *Serebryany Golub* ("The Silver Pigeon"). Russia is not the West, but neither is she the East: she is the immense "western East," played on by influences from either side. Therein lie her complexity and enigma.

History has verified Dostoievsky's gift of prophecy, but in its negative rather than its positive forecasts. In our day, fifty years after his death, it leaps to the eye that *The Possessed* was a truly prophetical work, but the positive prophecies scattered up and down the length of the *Diary of a Writer* have not been realized: to-day it is painful to read the pages in which he invokes the Russian Constantinople, the White Tzar, the Russians as the Christian people *par excellence*. On one particular point he was especially badly in error: he thought that the *intelligentzia* was defiled with godlessness and socialism but that the people would resist these temptations and remain faithful to the truth of Christ. That was an aberration of his religious populism, the fallaciousness and illusion of which have been demonstrated by the revolution. It is "the people" who have given up Christianity, while "the *intelligentzia*" is coming back to it. It is very important that the religious life of a people should never again be subordinated to a class point-of-view, a fault from which neither the slavophils nor Dostoievsky were free; on the contrary, appeal must be made to the personality and salvation sought in each one's spirit, and such proceeding is right in line with Dostoievsky's main spiritual direction. Slavophilism and Occidentalism are dead, and "populism" will never reappear in Russia under any form. The Russians now know a new dimension of being, and they have got to hammer out a new and more virile religious and national consciousness. Dostoievsky did a very great deal towards that work, and there can also be seen in him the temptations and errors that are to be avoided. If the Russian people is to attain spiritual rebirth and a new life it must tread the path of humiliation and despair and subject itself to a most severe discipline of the spirit. In no other way can it recover its spiritual power. Renunciation of messianic pretensions will strengthen the national vocation and the overthrow of populism will strengthen personality and make it worthy of its cultural and spiritual mission.

CHAPTER VIII

THE GRAND INQUISITOR. CHRIST AND ANTICHRIST

THE Legend of the Grand Inquisitor is the high point of Dostoievsky's work and the crown of his dialectic. It is in it that his constructive views on religion must be sought; all the tangles are unravelled and the radical problem, that of human freedom, is solved. This problem is more or less openly the theme of the whole Legend, and it is noteworthy that the extremely powerful vindication of Christ (which is what the Legend is) should be put into the mouth of the atheist Ivan Karamazov. It is indeed a puzzle, and it is not clear on the face of it which side the speaker is on and which side the writer; we are left free to interpret and understand for ourselves: that which deals with liberty is addressed to the free.

Every man is offered the alternatives of the Grand Inquisitor or of Jesus Christ and he must accept one or the other, for there is no third choice: what appear to be other solutions are only passing phases, variations on one or the other theme. In the Grand Inquisitor's system self-will leads to the negation and loss of freedom of spirit, which can be found

again in Christ alone. Dostoievsky's way of setting
this out is most admirable. His Christ is a shadowy
figure who says nothing all the time: efficacious religion does not explain itself, the principle of freedom
cannot be expressed in words; but the principle of
compulsion puts its case very freely indeed. In the
end, truth springs from the contradictions in the
ideas of the Grand Inquisitor, it stands out clearly
among all the considerations that he marshals
against it. He argues and persuades; he is a master of
logic and he is single-mindedly set on the carrying-
out of a definite plan: but our Lord's silence is
stronger and more convincing.

Two universal principles, then, confront one
another in the Legend: freedom and compulsion,
belief in the meaning of life and disbelief, divine love
and humanitarian pity, Christ and Antichrist. Dostoievsky makes an impressive figure of the Grand
Inquisitor. He is one of the "martyrs oppressed by a
great sorrow and loving mankind," an ascetic,
free from any material ambition, a man of one idea.
But he has a secret: he does not believe in God or in
any meaning of life which alone could give sense to
people's suffering in his name, and, having lost this
belief, he sees that large numbers of persons have not
the strength to bear the burden of freedom con-
ferred by Christ. Not believing in God, the Grand
Inquisitor also ceases to believe in man, for they are
two aspects of the same faith; Christianity is the reli-

gion of the God-man and therefore demands belief
in both God and man. But the idea of the God-man,
the uniting of the divine and human principles in
one freedom, is precisely the idea that the Grand
Inquisitor will not have; it is asking too much of man
to saddle him with this spiritual responsibility, he
must escape from Christian freedom and its burden
of discriminating and choosing between good and
evil. "Why distinguish these diabolical principles of
good and evil when to do so is the cause of so much
unhappiness?" A man can bear neither his own
sufferings nor those of other people, yet without
suffering there can be no liberty of choice, so we are
faced with a dilemma: on the one side, freedom; on
the other, contentment, well-being, rationalized
organization of life; either freedom with suffering or
contentment without freedom.

An overwhelming majority of people choose the
last. They give up the great ideas of God and immortality and freedom and come under the spell of a
fallacious love of one's neighbour in which God has
no part, a false compassion which promotes a godless
systematization of the world. The Grand Inquisitor
sets himself against God in the name of man, in the
name of the least of those individuals in whom he
believes no more than he does in God. That is an
important point. Those who devote themselves to
the earthly welfare of mankind rarely believe that
man is destined for a higher, a divine life. The

euclidian mind, full of revolt and self-limitation at the same time, tries to improve on the work of God. He created a universal order that is full of suffering and imposed on man the intolerable load of freedom and responsibility; in the euclidians' world there will be no suffering or responsibility—or freedom either. That mind necessarily leads to the Grand Inquisitor's system, the human ants' nest.

Freedom, he argues, is incompatible with happiness and should appertain only to a tiny aristocracy, and he accuses Christ of acting as if he did not love man when he imposed freedom on all. "Instead of taking away man's freedom thou didst increase it. Didst thou forget that man prefers peace and even death to freedom of choice of good or evil? Nothing is more attractive to him than freedom of conscience, but nothing causes him more suffering. And thou, instead of giving clear-cut rules that would have set man's conscience at rest once for all, thou didst put forward things that are unfamiliar, puzzling, and uncertain. . . . By so doing thou didst act as if thou didst not love mankind." If man is to be happy his conscience must be lulled, and that can be most easily done by taking away his freedom of choice; those who can cope with that freedom and move towards him who "did desire man's free love" are very few.

The Grand Inquisitor says that people "look less for God than for miracles," and the words well illus-

trate his poor opinion of human nature and lack of
faith in mankind. He reproaches our Lord accordingly: "Thou didst not come down [from the cross]
because thou wouldst not coerce man by a miracle:
thou didst crave for a free faith and not for one born
of marvels; thou didst crave for willing love, not the
obsequious raptures of slaves before the might that
has overawed them. But thou didst think too highly
of men: they are only slaves, even though rebellious
ones. . . . It was pitiless of thee to value [man] so
highly, for thou didst require far too much from him.
Hadst thou respected him less thou wouldst have
asked less, and that would have been more like love,
to have given him a lighter load. He is weak and
despicable." The aristocratism of Christ's religion
disturbs the Grand Inquisitor.

"Thou mayest well be proud of these children of
freedom, of their unconstrained love, of the glorious
sacrifice that they have freely made in thy name.
But remember, there were only some few thousands
of them, and they were as gods—what of the rest?
Are all those weak ones to blame that they could not
endure what the strong endured? Is a weak soul to
blame if it cannot take thy terrible gifts? Is it not
true that thou didst come only to the elect and for
the elect?" Thus does the Grand Inquisitor take up
the defence of enfeebled man and deprive him of
liberty in the name of love. "Did we not love mankind in that we meekly admitted its weakness and

wished lovingly to ease its yoke?" He says to Christ exactly what socialists are always saying to Christians: "Freedom and enough bread for all cannot go together, for men will never be able to share and share alike voluntarily. They will always be convinced, too, that they cannot be free, because they are weak, vicious, worthless, and rebellious. Thou didst promise them bread from Heaven, but can that compare with earthly bread in the eyes of this everlastingly sinful, thankless, and infirm human race? And if thousands and tens of thousands turn to thee for the sake of the heavenly bread, what is to become of the millions and tens of millions of those who will not have enough strength to forgo earthly bread for heavenly? Are we to believe that thou dost care only for the tens of thousands of great and strong, and that the millions of others, numerous as grains of sand on the shore, who are weak but yet worship thee, must exist only for the purposes of the great and strong? No, it is the weak that we are concerned for. . . . The spirit of the earth will rise up against thee in the name of this same earthly bread, it will overcome thee, and all will rally to it. . . . A new building, another and terrifying tower of Babel, will arise on the place of thy temple."

Christianity has always been reproved by atheistic socialism for not having made men happy and given them rest and fed them, and by preaching the religion of earthly bread socialism has attracted millions and

millions of followers. But, if Christianity has not
made men happy or given them rest or fed them, it
is because it has not wished to violate the freedom of
the human spirit, because it appeals to human freedom and awaits therefrom the fulfilling of the word
of Christ. Christianity is not to blame that mankind
has not willed the accomplishment of that word and
has betrayed it; the fault lies with man, not with the
God-man.

This terrible problem of liberty simply does not
exist for materialistic socialism; it expects to solve it
and achieve the liberation of man through a materialist and planned-out organization of life; its object
is to overthrow freedom and get rid of the irrational
element of life in the name of happiness, sufficiency,
and leisure. Men "will become free when they
renounce freedom. . . . We shall give them an unexciting modest happiness, suitable to the feeble creatures
that they are. We shall persuade them at last to
give up being proud, for thou didst lift them up and
thereby taught them pride. . . . Certainly we shall
make them work, but in their spare time we shall
organize their life like a children's game, with
children's songs and cantatas and innocent dances.
We shall allow them even sin, knowing that they are
so weak and helpless." The Grand Inquisitor promises that people shall be saved from "the great
anxiety and terrible agony they endure at present
in making a free decision for themselves. And all

these millions and millions of creatures will be happy. . . ." He has "left the proud and turned to the lowly for the happiness of the lowly," and to justify himself he appeals to the "tens of millions of beings who will never have known sin." Dostoievsky often returns to the notion of Christ's pride which is voiced by the Grand Inquisitor. In *A Raw Youth* somebody says of Versilov: "He is a very proud man, and many of these proud men believe in God, especially the most scornful ones. The reason is simple: they choose God rather than bow before men; to submit to him is less humiliating." Faith in God is a sign of high-mindedness, unbelief a symptom of superficiality. Ivan Karamazov understands the stupendous grandeur of the idea of God: "The astounding thing is that this notion of the necessity of God has been able to get a footing in the head of so wild and vicious an animal as man, so holy and moving and wise is it, and so honouring to the individual." If man has a higher nature and is called to a higher end it is because God exists, and man must believe in him; but if there be no God then neither is there a higher nature in man, and he must fall back into the social ant-heap whose principle is compulsion. A picture of this utopia can be seen in the Legend and in Shigalev's system, and everywhere else that man dreams of a future harmony for society.

In the three temptations presented to Christ "the

whole of the future history of mankind was foretold; they are the three forms in which all the historically insoluble contradictions of earthly human nature are reconciled." Our Lord refused them in the name of man's spiritual freedom, for it was not his will that the human spirit should be won over by bread, by an earthly kingdom, or by miracles. The Grand Inquisitor, on the contrary, welcomes them in the name of human happiness and contentment, and in welcoming them he renounces freedom. Especially does he approve the suggestion of Satan to turn stones into bread: "Thou didst reject the one banner that was offered thee that would have infallibly made all men bow down before thee alone—the banner of earthly bread; and thou didst reject it in the name of freedom and of a heavenly bread." The triumph of the three temptations will definitively mark man's attainment of content: "It was in thy power to have taught men all that they want to know on this earth, that is, to whom they must look up, to whom and how they can hand over their conscience, and how they can all join together and make a single unanimous common ant-heap of themselves, for the craving for a universal fusion is the third and last torment of man."

The Grand Inquisitor's mystery is that he is not working with Christ but with "him": "We are not with thee but with *the other*: that is our secret." This spirit that changes our Lord into Antichrist has appeared in history in various guises. For Dostoievsky the Catholic theocracy was one of them; it can be discerned in Byzantine Orthodoxy, in all Caesarism and all imperialism. A State that knows its limitations will not give expression to the Grand Inquisitor's ideas, nor will it strangle spiritual freedom. Throughout its history Christianity seems to have been constantly beset by the temptation to deny this liberty: nothing has been more difficult for Christians than to safeguard its integrity. So burdensome is the yoke of liberty to man that he has even tried to rid himself of it within Christianity itself. The principle of authority that plays so large a part in the history of the Church can easily be transformed into a denial of the mystery of Christian freedom, the mystery of Christ crucified. Truth nailed upon the cross compels nobody, oppresses no one; it must be accepted and confessed freely; its appeal is addressed to free spirits. Our Lord would not come down from the cross, as unbelievers called on him to do and still call on him to do, because he craved for "the free gift of love, not the obsequious raptures of slaves before the might that has overawed them."

A divine Truth panoplied in power, triumphant over the world and conquering souls, would not be consonant with the freedom of man's spirit, and so the mystery of Golgotha is the mystery of liberty; the

Son of God had to be crucified by the princes of this world in order that human freedom might be established and emphasized. The act of faith is an act of liberty, the world's unconstrained recognition of unseen things. Christ the Son of God, sitting at the right hand of the Father, can be seen only by a free act of faith, and he who so believes will witness the resurrection of the Crucified in glory. But the unbeliever, obsessed by the world of visible things, sees only the shameful punishment of a carpenter called Jesus, the downfall of one who had thought himself to be divine truth itself. There lies the whole secret of Christianity, and every time in history that man has tried to turn crucified Truth into coercive truth he has betrayed the fundamental principle of Christ.

Whenever this has happened churchmen have assumed the mask of earthly sovereignty and laid hands on the sword of Caesar. On the one hand, the organization of the Church takes on a juridical aspect and her life is subject to rules and regulations; on the other, her dogmatic system assumes a rationalist aspect: Christ's truth becomes subservient to logical constraint. Is that as much as to say that our Lord ought to have come down from the cross to make us believe? Throughout his passion and death there is no trace of any affirmation of logical or legal necessity. If we regard Christian truth rationally and juridically do we abandon freedom for compulsion? Dostoievsky said "yes." In face of the history of Christianity his faith in the free religion of Calvary was almost a new version of it, for all that he maintained the old traditional truths. It would seem that his conception of an unlimited freedom of spirit is not in accordance with traditional Christian teaching and, though it is much more acceptable to Eastern Orthodox than to Catholic notions, it was sufficiently revolutionary to frighten the more conservative Orthodox. Like all geniuses, Dostoievsky was an extremist; "safe" teachings are superficial teachings. The universality of a religious doctrine is a purely qualitative thing, without any reference to numbers: it may be more powerfully manifest in a small group than by millions of individuals, and a single religious genius can convey more by his excellence than a crowd by its size. Dostoievsky stood alone in his conception of Christian liberty, but he had the mark of universality none the less. His theories were akin to those of Khomiakov, and the Orthodoxy of these two was not the Orthodoxy of Metropolitan Philaret and of Theophanes the Hermit.

The ideas of the Grand Inquisitor appeal as much to the "left" as to the "right"; they are taken up by revolutionaries and socialists, by the Verhovenskys and the Shigalevs. The last-named supposes, "in view of a final solution of the problem, the division of mankind into two unequal parts. One-tenth is given personal freedom and unlimited rights over the remaining nine-tenths, who must be depersonalized and made like sheep; their primitive innocence will be regained through the unmeasured obedience exacted from them and they will live in a sort of Garden of Eden, except that they will have to work." The revolutionary Shigalev, like the Grand Inquisitor, is a fanatical "lover of humanity," and for both of them "slaves must be equal. Neither freedom nor equality can be had without despotism, but in a flock of sheep it is equality that must be supreme." It is true that equality is possible only under a despotism, and that is the end to which the prolonged agitation for equality is leading society, to the howling inequality of a tyranny of small groups.

Dostoievsky had an extremely inadequate and entirely exterior knowledge of Catholicism, and the Legend is directed much more against godless and materialist socialism, which is in full accord with the Grand Inquisitor's projected state of society. It is socialism that welcomes the temptations that Christ refused, especially that most dangerous one of changing stones into bread. The price of that miracle is loss of freedom, but socialism repudiates freedom for the sake of the contented happiness of the mob. And it worships a kingdom of this world, and the price of that also is loss of freedom, of spiritual freedom. Both systems are the fruit of disbelief in Truth and

Mind. If they do not exist, then there is only one worthy motive left to us, namely, sympathy for men in bulk, a wish to enable them to enjoy a little heedless pleasure during their short life. It should not be necessary to say that socialism is considered here as a new religion and not simply as a programme of social reforms or as an economic system, for in these it is possible that it may be justified.

The Grand Inquisitor, full of pity for man, a democrat, a socialist, is allured by evil masquerading as good. For the principle of Antichrist is not the old wickedness that springs to the eye in all its grossness: it is a new principle, refined, attractive, looking like goodness, and the superficial likeness between the evil antichristian principle and the good Christian principle is a source of great danger. The image of good begins to be "divided," Christ's image fades away and is merged into that of Antichrist. Men appear with divided minds—I have mentioned how the work of Merejkovsky reflects this confusion and uncertainty. Dostoievsky foresaw this state of mind, and his description of it was prophetical. When he has reached an extremity of inner division and is psychologically unbalanced, with all the customary landmarks wiped out and no new ones in sight, then man hears the call of Antichrist. There is a most noteworthy coincidence between the antichristian spirit as described by Dostoievsky, in the Legend and elsewhere, and as described by Vladimir Soloviev in his "Story about the Antichrist."* Soloviev also presents Antichrist as a humanitarian and a socialist who accepts the three temptations and aims at making men happy by devising an earthly paradise for them. An analogous description was given by Robert Hugh Benson in *Lord of the World*, wherein he shows presentiments and makes prophecies similar to those of Dostoievsky and Soloviev. (Incidentally, Benson's novel would have proved to Dostoievsky that all Catholics are not imbued with the spirit of the Grand Inquisitor!)

The development of Dostoievsky's dialectic depends on the antithesis of the God-man and the Superman, Christ and Antichrist, and human destiny is actualized in the clash between them. The discovery of the idea of self-deified man belongs to Dostoievsky, and it is worked out with special penetration in the person of Kirilov in *The Possessed*, who sets out the final problem of human destiny almost frenziedly: "The new man will come, happy and proud. He won't care whether he lives or doesn't live—he is the new man. He will overcome evil and suffering, he will be god—for there will no longer be any god. . . . God is the woeful thing that makes death frightening. The man who conquers pain and fear will himself be god. Then there will be new life, new men, new everything. . . . Man will be god and

* In *War, Progress and the End of History*. Translated by Alexander Bakshy. London, 1915.

his physical appearance will change.   The whole
world will be altered, things will be different,
thoughts, feelings, everything. . . . Whoever dares to
kill himself is god.   So anyone can bring about that
there should be no god and that nothing should
exist."   Kirilov does not believe in an eternal life to
come but in an endless life here and now; when
"time stops short it will be eternity," that is, when
"time is absorbed by the spirit."   He will "set a term
to the world" whose name will be "Superman."
"The God-man?" asks Stavroguin.   "No," answers
Kirilov, "the man-god, the super-man.   All the
difference is in that."   Deification of man ends collectively in the systems of Shigalev and the Grand
Inquisitor, individually in such spiritual experience
as that of Kirilov.   Kirilov wants to save man and
give him immortality, and for that end he offers
himself as a sacrifice: he kills himself.   But that death
is not a Christian death, a salvation-giving Calvary:
it differs from the death of our Lord at every point.
Christ fulfilled the will of the Father, Kirilov fulfils
his own will; Christ revealed eternal life in another
world, Kirilov wills eternal life in this; the path of
Christ was from Golgotha to the resurrection and
victory over death, Kirilov's ends in a death that
knows no resurrection: death is victorious over
deified man.   The only divine man who is not mortal
is Jesus Christ, but man sets himself at the opposite
pole to the God-man: he wants both to differ from

and be like him, and Dostoievsky gives us in Kirilov the ultimate result of this ambition. Like the Grand Inquisitor again, Kirilov is an ascetic and a person of high principles, and his story is worked out in a rare atmosphere of probity, but as usual Dostoievsky shows man's inner division leading to the superman and the consequent destruction of man's own image.

The Legend of the Grand Inquisitor contains the best of the constructive part of Dostoievsky's religious ideas; it is more coherent than the teaching of the Diary and of Zosima or Alyosha. The hidden image of Christ is akin to Nietzsche's Zarathustra: there is the same lofty spirit of freedom and aristocracy, and this last is an element of Dostoievsky's teaching which seems hitherto to have escaped notice. No one before him so strongly identified the image of Christ with a freedom of spirit that only a few can attain. This freedom is possible only because our Lord repudiated all temporal authority for himself. The will-to-power deprives of freedom both those who wield and those who are subject to it, and Christ knew no power except that of love, which alone is compatible with freedom. His is the religion of unconstrained love between God and man, and the attempts to actualize this in Christianity have generally been very far indeed from our Lord's own conception.

It is not only a conservative Catholicism but conservative Orthodoxy as well that finds the greatest difficulty in recognizing Dostoievsky as one of their own; his prophetical side and his search for a "new revelation" carried him beyond the bounds of historical Christianity.

The ideas found in the Diary do not do full justice to his religious views as a whole. In it a very recondite genius was trying to make himself comprehensible to the man-in-the-street, but really to enter into Dostoievsky's religious notions they must be looked at in an apocalyptic light, for he puts a problem in Christianity whose solution cannot be understood by reference to history alone. Zosima and Alyosha, in whom he gave voice to his positive theories, cannot be numbered among his best-drawn characters; Ivan Karamazov is infinitely more strong and convincing, and his very darkness is pierced by a shaft of strong light. It is not accidental that Dostoievsky removes his Father Zosima at the beginning of the book (*The Brothers Karamazov*), for he would hardle have been able to follow him up throughout its wholy length. Still, he succeeded in investing him with some of the characteristics of his new Christianity, with the result that Zosima by no means represents the traditional *staretz*; he does not, for example, resemble the Father Ambrose of the monastery of Optyna from whom he was drawn. Zosima knows something about the tragic destiny that Dostoievsky was discovering for man and he is marvellously understanding of the "karamazov" streak, of which the *staretzi* formed in the old school knew nothing. It is perfectly obvious that no living monk of Optyna would ever have said: "Brothers, do not fear men's sin but love them even in their sin, for then will your love resemble divine love and be greater than any other on earth. Love all God's creation, the whole of it and each tiny grain of sand. Love every leaf, every ray of God's light, love the animals, love the plants, love everything. Love all things, and you will find the mystery of God in all things. . . . Love to throw yourself upon the ground and kiss it. Kiss it and love it with a tireless, insatiable love. Love all men. Love all things. Seek this rapture and ecstasy. Water the earth with the tears of your joy and love those tears that you have shed. Don't be ashamed of such ecstasies but rather prize them, for they are a gift of God given not to all but to a few chosen ones."

Certainly such ecstasy was completely unknown to the *staretz* Ambrose; it recalls rather St. Francis of Assisi. But the land of Umbria is very different from the land of Russia; it grows different sorts of flowers, and this Umbrian blossom of universal holiness cannot be matched anywhere. Zosima was an expression of Dostoievsky's prophetical visions, visions which he did not succeed in representing in fully adequate forms. Only at the end of man's tragic journey was the new holiness to appear, and

Zosima becomes visible to the spirit of "underworld man," Raskolnikov, Stavroguin, Kirilov, Versilov, after the reign of the Karamazovs. But it is from the Karamazov world itself that the new man has to be born.

This birth of a new soul is described in the chapter of *The Brothers Karamazov* called "Cana of Galilee," where again there is more than a suggestion of the Christianity of St. John the Evangelist. After he has tasted the bitter anguish of death and decay Alyosha is blinded by the dazzling truth of the religion of the resurrection; he no longer sees the *staretz* Zosima in his coffin, the breath of corruption is blown away: he is called to the marriage-feast. "The little withered old man, his face covered with wrinkles, came towards him, laughing softly and happily. The coffin was gone, and he was dressed as he had been yesterday when he was sitting with them and the guests all around. His face was uncovered, his eyes shining. He, too, then was bidden to the feast, the wedding at Cana in Galilee." And when the old man says to him, "We are drinking the new wine, the wine of new and great gladness," resurrection is victorious over death in the soul o Alyosha and he is born again. "His enraptured soul was craving for freedom, space, openness. . . . The silence of earth seemed to melt in the silence of the heavens, the mystery of the world was joined with the mystery of the stars. . . . Alyosha stood gazing, and suddenly, as though his legs had given way, he threw himself to the ground. He did not know why he kissed it, why he had such an irresistible desire to embrace the whole of it. But kiss it he did, weeping and sobbing, watering it with his tears, passionately vowing to love it for ever, till the end of time. . . . But every moment he felt distinctly and as it were palpably that something certain and unshakable as the wheeling of the stars was entering into his soul. Some idea had laid hold upon him, and it would remain throughout his life and for ever and ever. He was a weak boy when he fell to the ground; he stood up a resolute life-long champion, and he felt and knew it all at once, at the very moment of his ecstasy."

Thus did Dostoievsky bring man's wanderings to a close: when he is separated from nature and the earth he is cast into hell, at the end of his course he comes back to them. But there is no such return for him who is wedded to self-will and rebellion, it is possible only by the way of Cana and Jesus Christ. The return is to a transfigured nature and a transfigured earth; the old nature and earth are closed to the man who has known self-will and inner division; there is no recovering a lost Eden, he must seek a new one.

The clash of the old "black" Christianity, rigid and superstitious, with the new "white" Christianity is embodied in Zosima's opponent, Father Ferapont, who represents religious torpor and death, while

Father Zosima stands for the resurrection of Orthodoxy and the emergence in her of new life. Confusion of the Holy Ghost with the holy spirit or holy
inspiration marks the definite capture of Ferapont's teaching by the powers of darkness, but
Alyosha's Christianity is Zosima's. Zosima says that
"Those who are apart from Christianity and in
revolt against it are none the less still personifica-
tions of Christ in their essence, and such they will
remain."   Such words, meaningless to Ferapont,
witness that Raskolnikov and Stavroguin and Kirilov
and Ivan Karamazov have not lost the image and
likeness of God completely: there is still time for them
to come back to Christ and they must journey by
Alyosha's road.

I personally know no more profoundly Christian
writer than Dostoievsky, and criticism of his religious
outlook touches only its surface. "Do you mean to
tell me," says Shatov to Stavroguin, "that if it were
mathematically proved that truth is not in Christ
you would adhere to him rather than to truth?" This
question might have been put to Dostoievsky and
he would have assented: indeed, he did, more than
once. Throughout his life he had an altogether
special and exclusive love for our Lord, and he was
certainly one of those who would reject truth in his
name rather than reject Christ himself—because he
saw that there is no truth except in him. The depth

of Dostoievsky's Christianity can be gauged above all
by his concern for man and his destiny: such a concern is possible only in a Christian conception of the
world and wherever found it demonstrates the
inward victory of Christ. This teaching stands out
even more clearly from his work in general than
from the teachings of Zosima and the *Diary of a
Writer* in particular. He pressed the consequences of
Christian anthropocentricity to their uttermost
limits. Religion penetrates to the spiritual depth of
man, but not after the manner of German mysticism
and idealism, which make man's form itself vanish
in the abyss of spirit and be lost in deity. Dostoievsky
emphasizes that the human form always persists, and
therein lies his specific Christianness. His Christian
metaphysic is best studied in the Legend of the Grand
Inquisitor, whose almost fathomless depth has never
yet been properly explored: it is a veritable revelation of Christian freedom.

Dostoievsky made much of the Russian Orthodox
theocratic idea, of "religious light coming from the
East." This is expressed in *The Brothers Karamazov*
and aspects of it recur in many parts of the *Diary of
a Writer*, so that to some it appears to be one of his
essential ideas. I cannot agree with them. It is not
particularly original and often conflicts with his
other religious notions, which are so eminently
"personalist." The theocratic idea belongs essen-

tially to the Old Testament, whence it was refracted into the Roman mind. Theocracy cannot but involve compulsion, and Vladimir Soloviev's "free theocracy" is a *contradictio in adiecto*; all the theocracies of history, pre-Christian and Christian, have been tyrannical; they have confounded the two orders of being, Heaven and earth, spirit and matter, Church and State. The theocratic idea is bound to come into conflict with Christian freedom, and in the Legend Dostoievsky dealt severe blows to this false theocratic notion of an earthly paradise, stigmatizing it as a deformation of itself. The freedom of Christ can be had only at the price of a renunciation of all claims to earthly power.

Nevertheless, Dostoievsky's own theocracy contained ill-assorted elements, things old and new. We find, for example, the Judaeo-Roman contention that the Church must be a temporal kingdom and we find the doctrines of St. Augustine; moreover, he had an inadequate idea of the independent temporal value of the State as a natural society directly ordained by God. The false anarchism involved in an unwillingness to admit any independent religious significance in the State is a thoroughly Russian characteristic, indicative of a national disease. It originates in the apocalypsism of the Russian mind which itself shows unhealthy symptoms of a want of spiritual manliness. In spite of Dostoievsky's prophecies, this apocalypsism has failed to resist the

o*—d

seductions of Antichrist: not the *intelligentzia* alone but "the people" have cheerfully given in to the "three temptations." Dostoievsky was the initial spiritual source of the apocalyptic-religious movement in Russia, all the varieties of neo-Christianity go back to him; he detected its besetting dangers and foresaw the coming of evil in new forms that would be difficult to see through. But he was not himself entirely proof against these deceits. His true teaching about man, his freedom and his destiny, is the permanent and invaluable part of his work.

CHAPTER IX

DOSTOIEVSKY AND US

THE intellectual and spiritual history of Russia in the nineteenth century is cut in two by Dostoievsky; between the slavophils and idealists of the earlier years of that century and the movements of the twentieth there was a spiritual revolution—and it was his work. A catastrophe divides contemporary Russia from the Russia of the 'forties, she lives in a new dimension unsuspected by the men who lived in those happier and more peaceful times. Not only does Russia of the present day belong to another historical era but also to an era weighed down by the consciousness of universal catastrophe, and this was inoculated into her by Dostoievsky. The men of a less disturbed period did not scent what was coming, and even such as Kireevsky, Khomiakov, and Aksakov, who had certain ideas in common with Dostoievsky and the Russians of to-day, were oblivious of the impending doom that was later to haunt such relatively serene and stable people as Prince Eugene Trubetzkoy. Westernizers like Odoyevsky and Stankievitch no more resembled the men of Dostoievsky's creation than did the slavophils, and though these parties were at war it would have been far easier for them to understand one another than to understand the men who came after Dostoievsky. One man might believe in God and another not, one might be a partizan of Russia and another of the West, yet one and the other belonged to the same psychic formation, had been woven on the same warp.   But the spiritual warp of Dostoievsky's disciples was different.   Their eyes were turned to an unknown but threatening future, apocalyptic waves broke over them, they were dashed from one extremity to its opposite; above all, they were to experience that inner division that the men of the 'forties did not undergo: to be sure, these were acquainted with discouragement and vexed dejection but they were better balanced, they did not experience an inner cleavage, neither did they see the Devil or study the problem of Antichrist any more than they lived in an atmosphere of apocalyptical obsession by the end of all things.   The word "apocalyptic" is susceptible of a psychological meaning and consequently of acceptance by those who repudiate its dogmatic religious significance, and no one will deny that the atmosphere of apocalypse that pervades Dostoievsky's work represents a trait fundamental in the Russian mind.

Ideologically the men of the 'forties were formed by Humanism; the Orthodoxy of the slavophils was full of it, and Khomiakov, with his remarkable con-

ception of the Church, was a Christian humanist.
But the man whom Humanism treated as a being in
three dimensions became for Dostoievsky a being in
four, and in the new dimension were those irrational
elements which upset the truths of Humanism. New
worlds were opened in man, the whole perspective
was changed, for the depths of human nature had
not been reached either by the superficial materialistic Humanism or by the more penetrating idealistic
Humanism or even by Christian Humanism: there
was too much dreaming and illusion in all of it.
The realism of real life, as Dostoievsky used to say,
the reality of human nature, are more tragic and
contain contradictions that never reached humanist
consciousness. There can be no more humanists (in
the old sense of the word) and no more "Schillerism"
after Dostoievsky—we are all doomed to be tragic
realists. This tragic realism is the mark of an age
which lays on us so heavy a responsibility that the
men of the last generation could hardly have borne
it. It was in their time that "those cursed questions"
became real and vital, matters of life and death in
which both particular and general destinies were involved. If the thinking part of the generation which
experienced the sharpening of these questions at the
beginning of the twentieth century seemed sometimes
to fail in its spiritual task, if one is sometimes struck
by the faultiness of its moral character, it is precisely
because everything had become so momentous, so

real in the ontological sense—we expect more from
them than from their predecessors of sixty years
before.

When at the beginning of the twentieth century a
stream of spiritual and religious ideas gushed out
and flowed in a contrary direction to the positivism
and materialism of the traditional thought of the
Russian *intelligentzia*, its representatives, Rosanov,
Merejkovsky, the neo-idealists, Leo Shestov, Biely,
Vyacheslav Ivanov, all put themselves under the
standard of Dostoievsky: they were children of his
mind and set themselves to solve the problems that
he had set. Tolstoy may seem to take up more room
on the stage, but Dostoievsky had the wider and
stronger influence. Tolstoy was by far the more
"get-at-able" and the easier to take for one's
"master," he was, moreover, more of a moralist;
whereas in the furrow ploughed by Dostoievsky it
was the complex and keen Russian metaphysical
thought that grew and had to be mastered. People
may be divided into two types: those who are drawn
to Tolstoy's mind and those drawn to Dostoievsky's,
and we shall find that the "tolstoyans" have great
difficulty in understanding Dostoievsky properly;
not only that, but they often dislike him. Those
who are satisfied by Tolstoy's rationalism and
monism do not appreciate the tragic contradictions
of such works as *The Possessed*: they are frightened by

the writer's spirit, which seems to them antichristian. Tolstoy, to whom the idea of the Redemption was quite foreign and who lacked any personal feeling for our Lord, is their representative figure of an authentic Christian, faithful to the word of the gospel; Dostoievsky, who loved Christ consumingly and was immersed in the mystery of his atonement, him they regard as an unchristian, gloomy, disturbing writer who opens the pits of hell. There is an unbridgeable gap, over which the holders of two differing fundamental conceptions of existence face one another.

Anyway, so far as creative religious thought is concerned, Tolstoy has been almost barren while Dostoievsky's work has been exceedingly fruitful. The Shatovs, Kirilovs, Verhovenskys, Stavroguins, and Ivans who in Dostoievsky's day belonged only to the realm of prophecy have all appeared in the world of physical reality during the past forty years; his essential themes, only latent in the 'seventies, came to life in the first and little and in the second and great Russian revolutions. There one comes into contact with the religious structure of "revolutionaryism" in Russia and sees its lack of political impulse. The revolution brought Dostoievsky nearer to his fellow-citizens and, whereas the other great Russian writers were pre-revolutionary, he may be called a writer of the revolutionary period. The coming revolution that he foretold fascinated him in his work, and he constantly spoke of it as a manifestation of the spirit; he was a manifestation of the spirit himself and all that he foresaw is here: the era of the "cursed questions," of developed psychology, of revolt of underworld individualism, rejecting any fixed mode of life, parallel with its contrary, the revolt of impersonal collectivism. All that is found at the bottom of the revolutionary stream, where too we can meet Shigalev and Verhovensky, Stavroguin and Kirilov, Ivan Karamazov and Smerdyakov. Dostoievsky created prototypes. His psychology never stopped at the psycho-physical surface of life, and that is why Tolstoy is the better psychologist in the narrow and exact sense of the word; Dostoievsky's science dealt with the life not of the soul but of the spirit, and it was extended to God and to Satan. And these are the questions, ultimate matters, that Russia has long been interested in, as well as in the psychological ones. The destinies of the revolution and of social life are subordinate to a solution of the problems of God and Satan, and it was Dostoievsky who got us out of the vicious circle of merely psychological research. Shestov was wrong to regard him as a psychologist of the underworld soul; the life of even the lower regions of the soul were for him only a step in man's spiritual journey, and he took us beyond it. Throughout this book I have tried to show that Dostoievsky was not only a great artist but the greatest of Russia's metaphysicians. Ideas

are man's daily bread: he cannot live without pon-
dering the questions of God, Satan, immortality,
freedom, evil, the destiny of mankind; it is essential
that he should do so, for if there be no immortality
life is not worth the trouble of living. Accordingly,
Dostoievsky's metaphysic is not abstract; he taught
us Russians that ideas are living, concrete, substan-
tial things and we are now all his spiritual children,
anxious to put and solve metaphysical problems in
the same spirit that he put and solved them. Soloviev
was not concrete, he combated an abstract metaphysic in an abstract way, and consequently Dostoievsky gets nearer to the problems. It is true that
Soloviev approaches very close to him and sometimes,
especially on the subject of Antichrist, they are at
one, but they are parallel manifestations. Soloviev
was not a disciple of Dostoievsky. Now Rosanov
was, and he was also one of the most notable writers
of the beginning of this century. His style alone is
astounding, and appears to derive directly from some
of the characters in Dostoievsky's novels; he had the
same sense of the concrete and living substance of
metaphysics and dealt with the same themes as his
master. But he is a sign of the dangers that are latent
in Dostoievsky's thought: one can sometimes hear
behind his words the voice of Fyodor Pavlovitch
Karamazov—who has climbed on to a pedestal of
genius! The complete absence of any spiritual self-
control in Rosanov shows that the influence of

Dostoievsky can be a source of weakness. The ideology of Merejkovsky, too, was born of the spirit of Dostoievsky; its source was in the "Cana of Galilee" episode and the doctrine of the God-man and the superman. But this influence did not enable Merejkovsky to find the criterion by which Christ can be distinguished from Antichrist, and his mind remained "divided." That fact suggests a last question: Can Dostoievsky be taken as a master and guide?

Dostoievsky revealed many things to us and taught us a great deal; we are all his spiritual heirs, but he does not teach us how to live, in the strict sense. There are dangers in his spiritual truths and to draw a lesson in life from them is a perilous experiment. The Russian soul is dangerously intoxicated, it has a thirst for self-destruction, for losing itself; in it the instinct of self-preservation is very underdeveloped, and therefore one cannot safely encourage it to follow the tragic way through inner division and darkness. Without doubt the human tragedy that Dostoievsky revealed can be a valuable and beneficial experience, but it must not be set before man as a road to be followed. Its dionysism and exaltation may be regarded as an original endowment of man, a foundation of being, the environment in which our destiny is worked out, but its intemperate |atmosphere must not be made the norm. Moreover, to interpret Dostoievsky as a normal influence would be as dangerous as it would be difficult, as I have already pointed out when speaking of his conception of evil. It is therefore extremely important to find out exactly how his teaching should be looked at.

Dostoievsky's work is evidence both of the immense spiritual possibilities latent among the Russians and of the fact that they are spiritually sick; no Western people has found it so difficult to discipline its own spirit. "Spinelessness" must be considered one of their national faults, and the achievement of moral character and a spiritual manliness is therefore a vital and most pressing problem for them. Has Dostoievsky helped towards this end? I have tried to show how strong his enthusiasm for freedom of spirit was, but he did not tell us how it is to be acquired, how we may attain spiritual and moral autonomy, how as individuals and as a people we can emancipate ourselves from base influences; he taught all about freedom as the first principle of life but he was not a "Professor of Freedom." For him man's only road is through tragedy, inner division, the abyss, the attainment of light through darkness, and his greatness lay in that he showed the light shining in the darkness. But unfortunately the Russian is inclined to jump into the dark waters and stop there as long as possible; he has a strong sense of personality and personal destiny but seems unable

to defend himself from the destructive attacks of
dionysiac passions. Dostoievsky reflects the Russian
entangled in the elementary activities of the soul,
and he found out important things about his spirit
and the human spirit at large; but he never set forth
spiritual maturity, the spirit controlling the chaotic
movements of the soul and directing it to higher
ends. So far as personality is concerned he did not
escape from that fatal state of inner division: he
accorded to personality an exclusive value, but he
also believed in the universal and the "collective."
His religious populism paralyses personal responsibility and spiritual self-discipline. Among Russians
the idea of religious universality is often found to be
only a false idealization of "the people" as sole cus-
todians of the spirit. Dostoievsky was their greatest
genius, but they have not acquired a healthy and
mature national consciousness since he appeared
among them, as the revolution has shown in a most
cruel fashion. What Fichte and men like him did
for the Germans has yet to be accomplished for the
Russians: effective ideas of responsibility, self-discipline, and spiritual autonomy have still to be
given to them. The contradiction in his thought pre-
vented Dostoievsky from being the needed reformer;
he set himself to the task with one side of his being,
but the other, corrupted by populism and collectivism, stood in the way of his success.

The Russian dislike for "average culture" found

expression in Dostoievsky, but he represented the
universal crisis of culture as well. Culture is an
environment, there is neither beginning nor end
to its aspirations, but it does not attain or actualize
true being: it is not ontological but symbolic. The
crisis of culture is indeed the crisis of its symbolism,
and it weighs particularly heavily on the "symbolists." One might hazard the paradox that
"Symbolism" is the desire to overcome symbolism,
to transform culture as symbolical into culture as
ontological, that is, to find in it not symbols of ultimate reality but that reality itself. True symbolists
then are the true realists, for they know that the
culture in which "realists" remain so innocently
shut up is a matter only of symbols; the mind must
go behind them to find reality. The crisis of culture
is also a longing to escape from compromise into
some destructive certainty; it therefore has the
apocalyptic tendency that was noticeable in Nietzsche but far more strongly in Dostoievsky.

Distrust of and even hostility towards average
culture, the need for an ultimate end, apocalyptic
leanings: these are thoroughly Russian dispositions,
the source of their spiritual eccentricity and unhealthiness, and refusal of average culture was
carried to a point where it became dangerous, a sign
of nihilism. Cultural bankruptcy meant one thing
for Dostoievsky and quite another for those of his
countrymen who had only a semi- or sub-culture.

Among the intellectual *élite* he awoke a desire to put
aside cultural symbols for veritable realities, but his
effect on the others was to paralyse all leanings towards culture and so to strengthen the nihilist point
of view. The Russian gladly rids himself of all cultural trappings in the hope that in the "state of
nature" true being may be revealed to him; of course
it is not, because culture is in fact the way that leads
to the reality of being: divine life itself is the highest
culture of the spirit. The influence in this matter of
Tolstoy upon Russia was deplorable; Dostoievsky's,
like that of all the great national writers, was mixed,
but if he precipitated a crisis of culture he was not its
enemy, as Tolstoy was. Dostoievsky joined a sense
of history and its continuity, an appreciation of its
survivals and values, with his apocalyptic element,
and it is to be wished that the Russians would
realize themselves as his heirs in that respect.

If Dostoievsky cannot be considered a master of
spiritual discipline, if we even have to overcome
first "psychologism" and then "dostoievskyism" in
ourselves, yet there is at least one matter on which
his teaching remains definite and valid for all: he
showed that the light in our darkness is Christ, that
the most abandoned individual still retains God's
image and likeness, that we must love such an one as
our neighbour and respect his freedom. Dostoievsky
takes us into very dark places but he does not let

darkness have the last word; his books do not leave
us with an impression of sombre and despairing
pessimism, because with the darkness there goes a
great light. Christ is victorious over the world and
irradiates all. Dostoievsky's Christianity was light-
bearing, the Christianity of St. John, and he con-
tributed towards the religion that is to come, the
religion of freedom and love, the definitive triumph
of Christ's eternal gospel.

There are plenty of dead things in Christianity,
and their putrefaction spreads pestilence that can
poison the well-springs of life. In some respects
Christians are more like minerals than parts of a
living organism: we are petrified, dead words come
out from our lifeless mouths. "The Spirit breatheth
where he will," and he will not breathe upon souls
that are religiously desiccated: they must be first
remade and baptized anew, but with fire. Progress
of the antichristian spirit, loss of faith, spread of
materialism, these are only secondary results, consequences of the stiffening and death that has gone
on within Christianity, in the lives of Christians. A
Christianity given over to stereotyped rhetoric, formal and spiritless in its rites, debased by clericalism
or laicizing, cannot be a life-giving force. Yet it is
from Christianity that regeneration and renewal of
the spirit must come; if it is truly the timeless and
eternal religion, then it has to be the religion of the
new age that is upon us, and there must arise within

her a creative movement such as the world has not known for a long time.

Dostoievsky prepared souls for this remaking and fiery baptism: he sweetened the ground for a spiritual renaissance in which the new and eternal covenant, living Christianity, should be made manifest. Far more than Tolstoy, he deserves the name of a religious reformer. Tolstoy destroyed the values of Christianity and tried to set up a religion of his own; the services he rendered were only negative and open to criticism, while Dostoievsky invented no new religion but was faithful to Christian truth and its eternal tradition. He inspired them with fresh spirit and brought to Christians a creative impetus that would not be gainsaid; he invoked St. John's Apocalypse and turned their eyes to the future, at a time when they were living almost entirely in the past. Dostoievsky's work has been extraordinarily fruitful as a prophetical presentation of the highest spiritual possibilities. But at the same time, as we have already seen, this work shared the inner division which belongs to the Russian character, the imprint of whose powers and weaknesses it bears. Russians must labour spiritually in his footsteps, learning from his experience to know and to purify themselves.

Western Europe to-day, caught by a tide of disaster, is very conscious of Dostoievsky, and she is more able than she was to understand him. Fate has

jerked her out of that state of middle-class self-satisfaction in which, up to the time of the world war, she
obviously hoped to stop for ever. For a long time
European society had stayed at the fringes of being
and was content with an outward existence; it was
happy to remain established on the surface of things
till the end of time. But the subsoil of this bourgeois
Europe was discovered to be volcanic and deep and,
after certain terrible surface disturbances such as the
war and the Russian revolution, this discovery was
followed by a movement towards the newly-found
spiritual depths. In the midst of their calamities
people in the West heard an echo of this depth
within them and, under irresistible impulse and by
sure instinct, turned to the great Russian and
universal genius who had first explored the inward
abysses of man and foretold a catastrophe for the
world.

So great is the worth of Dostoievsky that to have
produced him is by itself sufficient justification for
the existence of the Russian people in the world;
and he will bear witness for his countrymen at the
last judgment of the nations.

A BRIEF OVERVIEW OF
NIKOLAI BERDYAEV'S LIFE AND WORKS

Nikolai Berdyaev (1874–1948) was one of the greatest religious thinkers of the 20th century. His adult life, led in Russia and in western European exile, spanned such cataclysmic events as the Great War, the rise of Bolshevism and the Russian Revolution, the upsurge of Nazism, and the Second World War. He produced profound commentaries on many of these events, and had many acute things to say about the role of Russia in the evolution of world history. There was sometimes almost no separation between him and these events: for example, he wrote the book on Dostoevsky while revolutionary gunfire was rattling outside his window.

Berdyaev's thought is primarily a religious metaphysics, influenced not only by philosophers like Kant, Hegel, Schopenhauer, Solovyov, and Nietzsche, but also by religious thinkers and mystics such as Meister Eckhart, Angelus Silesius, Franz van Baader, Jakob Boehme, and Dostoevsky. The most fundamental concept of this metaphysics is that of the *Ungrund* (a term taken from Boehme), which is the pure potentiality of being, the negative ground essential for the realization of the novel, creative aspects of existence. A crucial element of Berdyaev's thought is his philosophical anthropology: A human being is originally an "ego" out which a "person" must develop. Only when an ego freely acts to realize its own concrete essence, rather than abstract or arbitrary goals, does it become a person. A society that furthers the goal of the development of egos into persons is a true community, and the relation then existing among its members is a sobornost.

He showed an interest in philosophy early on, at the age of fourteen reading the works of Kant, Hegel, and Schopenhauer.

228

While a student at St. Vladimir's University in Kiev, he began to participate in the revolutionary Social-Democratic movement and to study Marxism. In 1898, he was sentenced to one month in a Kiev prison for his participation in an anti-government student demonstration, and was later exiled for two years (1901–02) to Vologda, in the north of Russia.

His first book, *Subjectivism and Individualism in Social Philosophy* (1901), represented the climax of his infatuation with Marxism as a methodology of social analysis, which he attempted to combine with a neo-Kantian ethics. However, as early as 1903, he took the path from "Marxism to idealism," which had already been followed by such former Marxists as Peter Struve, Sergey Bulgakov, and S. L. Frank. In 1904 Berdyaev became a contributor to the philosophical magazine *New Path*. The same year he married Lydia Trushcheva, a daughter of a Petersburg lawyer. In 1905–06, together with Sergey Bulgakov, he edited the magazine *Questions of Life*, attempting to make it the central organ of new tendencies in the domains of socio-political philosophy, religious philosophy, and art. The influence exerted upon him by the writers and philosophers Dmitry Merezhkovsy and Zinaida Gippius, during meetings with them in Paris in the winter of 1907–08, led him to embrace the Russian Orthodox faith. After his return to Russia, he joined the circle of Moscow Orthodox philosophers united around the Path publishing house (notably Bulgakov and Pavel Florensky) and took an active part in organizing the religious-philosophical Association in Memory of V. Solovyov. An important event in his life at this time was the publication of his article "Philosophical Truth and the Truth of the Intelligentsia" in the famous and controversial collection *Landmarks* (1909), which subjected to a critical examination the foundations of the world-outlook of the left-wing Russian intelligentsia. Around this time, Berdyaev published a work which inaugurated his life-long exploration of the concept of freedom in its many varieties and ramifications. In *The Philosophy of Freedom* (1911), a critique of the "pan-gnoseologism" of recent German and Russian philosophy led Berdyaev to a search for an authentically Christian ontology. The end result of this search was a philosophy of freedom, according to which human beings are rooted in a sobornost of being and thus possess true knowledge.

In 1916, Berdyaev published the most important work of his early period: *The Meaning of the Creative Act*. The originality of this work is rooted in the rejection of theodicy as a traditional problem of the Christian consciousness, as well as in a refusal to accept the view that creation and revelation have come to an end and are complete. The central element of the "meaning of the creative act" is the idea that man reveals his true essence in the course of a continuing creation realized jointly with God (a theurgy). Berdyaev's notion of "theurgy" (in contrast to those of Solovyov and Nikolai Fyodorov) is distinguished by the inclusion of the element of freedom: the creative act is a means for the positive self-definition of freedom not as the choice and self-definition of persons in the world but as a "foundationless foundation of being" over which God the creator has no power.

Berdyaev's work from 1914 to 1924 can be viewed as being largely influenced by his inner experience of the Great War and the Russian Revolution. His main themes during this period are the "cosmic collapse of humanity" and the effort to preserve the hierarchical order of being (what he called "hierarchical personalism"). Revolutionary violence and nihilism were seen to be directly opposed to the creatively spiritual transformation of "this world" into a divine "cosmos." In opposing the chaotic nihilism of the first year of the Revolution, Berdyaev looked for support in the holy ontology of the world, i.e., in the divine cosmic order. The principle of hierarchical inequality, which is rooted in this ontology, allowed him to nullify the main argument of the leveling ideology and praxis of Communism—the demand for "social justice." Berdyaev expressed this view in his *Philosophy of Inequality* (1923).

During this period, Berdyaev posed the theme of Russian

messianism in all its acuteness. Torn apart by the extremes of apocalyptic yearning and nihilism, Russia is placed into the world as the "node of universal history" (the "East-West"), in which are focused all the world's problems and the possibility of their resolution, in the eschatological sense. In the fall of the monarchy in February 1917, Berdyaev saw an opportunity to throw off the provincial Russian empire which had nothing in common with Russia's messianic mission. But the Russian people betrayed the "Russian idea" by embracing the falsehood of Bolshevism in the October Revolution. The Russian messianic idea nevertheless remains true in its ontological core despite this betrayal.

In the fall of 1919, Berdyaev organized in Moscow the Free Academy of Spiritual Culture, where he led a seminar on Dostoevsky and conducted courses on the Philosophy of Religion and the Philosophy of History. This latter course became the basis of one of his most important works: *The Meaning of History: An Essay on the Philosophy of Human Destiny* (1923). His attacks against the Bolshevik regime became increasingly intense: he called the Bolsheviks nihilists and annihilators of all spiritual values and culture in Russia. His activities and statements, which made him a notable figure in post-revolutionary Moscow, began to attract the attention of the Soviet authorities. In 1920, he was arrested in connection with the so-called "tactical center" affair, but was freed without any consequences. In 1922, he was arrested again, but this time he was expelled from Russia on the so-called "philosopher's ship" with other ideological opponents of the regime such as Bulgakov, Frank, and Struve.

Having ended up in Berlin, Berdyaev gradually entered the sphere of post-War European philosophy; he met Spengler, von Keyserling, and Scheler. His book *The New Middle Ages: Reflections on the Destiny of Russia and Europe* (1924) (English title: *The End of Our Time*) brought him European celebrity. Asserting that modern history has come to an end, and that it has been a failure, Berdyaev again claimed that Russia (now the post-revolutionary one) had a messianic mission. He wrote that "culture is now not just European; it is becoming universal. Russia, which had stood at the center of East and West, is now—even if by a terrible and catastrophic path—acquiring an increasingly palpable world significance, coming to occupy the center of the world's attention" (*The New Middle Ages*, p. 36). In 1924, Berdyaev moved to Paris, where he became a founder and professor of the Russian Religious-Philosophical Academy. In 1925, he helped to found and became the editor of the Russian religious-philosophical journal *Put'* (*The Path*), arguably the most important Russian religious journal ever published. He organized interconfessional meetings of representatives of Catholic, Protestant, and Orthodox religious-philosophical thought, with the participation of such figures as Maritain, Mounier, Marcel, and Barth.

In the émigré period, his thought was primarily directed toward what can be called a liberation from ontologism. Emigration became for him an existential experience of "rootless" extra-hierarchical existence, which can find a foundation solely in "the kingdom of the Spirit," i.e., in the person or personality. The primacy of "freedom" over "being" became the determining principle of his philosophy, a principle which found profound expression in his book *On the Destiny of Man: An Essay on Paradoxical Ethics* (1931), which he considered his "most perfect" book. This is how he expressed this principle: "creativeness is possible only if one admits freedom that is not determined by being, that is not derivable from being. Freedom is rooted not in being but in 'nothingness'; freedom is foundationless, is not determined by anything, is found outside of causal relations, to which being is subject and without which being cannot be understood" (from his autobiography, the Russian version, *Self-knowledge*, p. 231).

At around the same time, Berdyaev re-evaluated Kant's philosophy, arriving at the conclusion that only this philosophy "contains the foundations of a true metaphysics." In particular, Kant's "recognition that there is a deeper reality hidden behind the world of phenomena" helped Berdyaev formulate a key principle of his personalism: the doctrine of "objectification," which he first systematically developed in *The World of Objects: An Essay on the Philosophy of Solitude and Social Intercourse* (1934) (English title: *Solitude and Society*). This is how Berdyaev explained this doctrine: "Objectification is an epistemological interpretation of the fallenness of the world, of the state of enslavement, necessity, and disunitedness in which the world finds itself. The objectified world is subject to rational knowledge in concepts, but the objectification itself has an irrational source" (*Self-knowledge*, p. 292). Using man's creative powers, it is possible to pierce this layer of objectification, and to see the deeper reality. Man's "ego" (which knows only the objectified world) then regains its status of "person," which lives in the non-objectified, or real, world. Berdyaev had a strong sense of the unreality of the world around him, of his belonging to another—real—world.

After the Second World War, Berdyaev's reflections turned again to the role of Russia in the world. His first post-war book was *The Russian Idea: The Fundamental Problems of Russian Thought of the 19th Century and the Beginning of the 20th Century* (1946), in which he tried to discover the profound meaning of Russian thought and culture. Himself being one of the greatest representatives of this thought and culture, he saw that the meaning of his own activity was to reveal to the western world the distinctive elements of Russian philosophy, such as its existential nature, its eschatalogism, its religious anarchism, and its obsession with the idea of "Divine humanity."

Berdyaev is one of the greatest religious existentialists. His philosophy goes beyond mere thinking, mere rational conceptualization, and tries to attain authentic life itself: the profound layers of existence that touch upon God's world. He directed all of his efforts, philosophical as well as in his personal and public life, at replacing the kingdom of this world with the kingdom of God. According to him, we can all attempt to do this by tapping the divine creative powers which constitute our true nature. Our mission is to be collaborators with God in His continuing creation of the world.

Summing up his thought in one sentence, this is what Berdyaev said about himself: "Man, personality, freedom, creativeness, the eschatological-messianic resolution of the dualism of two worlds—these are my basic themes."

BORIS JAKIM
2009

BIBLIOGRAPHY OF NIKOLAI BERDYAEV'S
BOOKS IN ENGLISH TRANSLATION
(IN ALPHABETICAL ORDER)

The Beginning and the End. Russian edition 1947. First English edition 1952.

The Bourgeois Mind and Other Essays. English edition 1934.

Christian Existentialism. A Berdyaev Anthology. 1965.

Christianity and Anti-Semitism. Russian edition 1938. First English edition 1952.

Christianity and Class War. Russian edition 1931. First English edition 1933.

The Destiny of Man. Russian edition 1931. First English edition 1937.

The Divine and the Human. Russian edition 1952. First English edition 1947.

Dostoevsky: An Interpretation. Russian edition 1923. First English edition 1934.

Dream and Reality: An Essay in Autobiography. Russian edition 1949. First English edition 1950.

The End of Our Time. Russian edition 1924. First English edition 1933.

The Fate of Man in the Modern World. First Russian edition 1934. English edition 1935.

Freedom and the Spirit. Russian edition 1927. First English edition 1935.

Leontiev. Russian edition 1926. First English edition 1940.

The Meaning of History. Russian edition 1923. First English edition 1936.

The Meaning of the Creative Act. Russian edition 1916. First English edition 1955.

The Origin of Russian Communism. Russian edition 1937. First English edition 1937.

The Realm of Spirit and the Realm of Caesar. Russian edition 1949. First English edition 1952.

The Russian Idea. Russian edition 1946. First English edition 1947.

Slavery and Freedom. Russian edition 1939. First English edition 1939.

Solitude and Society. Russian edition 1934. First English edition 1938.

Spirit and Reality. Russian edition 1946. First English edition 1937.

Towards a New Epoch. Transl. from the original French edition 1949.

Truth and Revelation. English edition 1954.